T0031785

A gift for

....

From

....

Date

....

GOD'S
PROMISES®

DURING TIMES OF TROUBLE

JACK COUNTRYMAN

COUNTRYMAN®

An Imprint of Thomas Nelson Publishers

THOMAS NELSON
Since 1798

God's Promises During Times of Trouble

© 2023 Jack Countryman

Published in Nashville, Tennessee, by Thomas Nelson. JCountryman® is a registered trademark of Thomas Nelson. Thomas Nelson is a registered trademark of HarperCollins Christian Publishing, Inc.

Thomas Nelson titles may be purchased in bulk for educational, business, fundraising, or sales promotional use. For information, please e-mail SpecialMarkets@ThomasNelson.com.

Unless otherwise noted, Scripture quotations are taken from the New King James Version®. Copyright © 1982 by Thomas Nelson. Used by permission. All rights reserved.

Scripture quotations marked CEB are taken from the Common English Bible. Copyright © 2011 Common English Bible.

Scripture quotations marked CEV are taken from the Contemporary English Version. Copyright © 1991, 1992, 1995 by American Bible Society. Used by permission.

Scripture quotations marked ESV are taken from the ESV® Bible (The Holy Bible, English Standard Version®). Copyright © 2001 by Crossway, a publishing ministry of Good News Publishers. Used by permission. All rights reserved.

Scripture quotations marked MSG are taken from THE MESSAGE. Copyright © 1993, 2002, 2018 by Eugene H. Peterson. Used by permission of NavPress. All rights reserved. Represented by Tyndale House Publishers, a Division of Tyndale House Ministries.

Scripture quotations marked NASB are taken the New American Standard Bible® (NASB). Copyright © 1960, 1962, 1963, 1968, 1971, 1972, 1973, 1975, 1977, 1995, 2020 by The Lockman Foundation. Used by permission. www.Lockman.org.

Scripture quotations marked NIV are taken from The Holy Bible, New International Version®, NIV®. Copyright © 1973, 1978, 1984, 2011 by Biblica, Inc.® Used by permission of Zondervan. All rights reserved worldwide. www.Zondervan.com. The "NIV" and "New International Version" are trademarks registered in the United States Patent and Trademark Office by Biblica, Inc.®

Scripture quotations marked NLV are taken from the New Life Version. © 1969, 2003 by Barbour Publishing, Inc.

Scripture quotations marked NLT are taken from the Holy Bible, New Living Translation. Copyright © 1996, 2004, 2015 by Tyndale House Foundation. Used by permission of Tyndale House Ministries, Carol Stream, Illinois 60188. All rights reserved.

Scripture quotations marked TLB are taken The Living Bible. Copyright © 1971. Used by permission of Tyndale House Publishers, a Division of Tyndale House Ministries, Carol Stream, Illinois 60188. All rights reserved.

ISBN 978-1-4003-3428-5 (audio download)
ISBN 978-1-4003-3427-8 (eBook)
ISBN 978-1-4003-3426-1 (softcover)

Library of Congress Cataloging-in-Publication Data on File

Printed in India

23 24 25 26 27 REP 6 5 4 3 2 1

CONTENTS

GOD PROMISES YOU HIS WORD OF TRUTH

So many times in life, we are faced with challenges and disappointments. Thankfully, God has given us His encouraging words of Scripture to give us answers when we are facing these difficult times. *God's Promises® During Times of Trouble* shares God's promises and truths to offer comfort and peace when times are hard.

As you go through this book, you will find ten sections, each containing five topics to help you navigate life's trials and tribulations. *God's Promises® During Times of Trouble* is filled with content to help you deal with life's challenges. In this edition, we have included inspirational quotes from outstanding Christian authors that speak to your needs when you feel like life is out of control.

In today's noisy world, with its myriad voices calling you in different directions, it is easy to find yourself confused. The loud and contradictory message of the world speaks—about your values and purpose, about what to believe, and about how to live—and can sometimes cause uncertainty about specific situations and who you are in general. By God's grace, He has provided His Word of truth. You can open the pages of Scripture in this book and find all the answers you need to honor God with what you say and do.

Take time to get away from the noise of life and spend time alone with God, reading and believing His promises to you. He will direct your path toward peace and contentment and clarity—gifts that only He can give. We pray that by spending time in God's Word, you will find the answers you need in life, and that God will give you His peace that passes all understanding.

"But you, when you pray, go into your room, and when you have shut your door, pray to your Father who is in the secret place; and your Father who sees in secret will reward you openly. And when you pray, do not use vain repetitions as the heathen do. For they think that they will be heard for their many words. "Therefore do not be like them. For your Father knows the things you have need of before you ask Him."

MATTHEW 6:6-8

SCRIPTURE OVERFLOWS WITH GOD'S PROMISES

RICK WARREN ON GOD'S WORD

Jesus said, "You will know the truth, and the truth will set you free" (John 8:32 NIV). When you base your life on truth—when you live with the right kind of thoughts, not misconceptions or false beliefs, and you base your life on right thoughts out of God's Word—you will be set free. You will find your old habits, feelings, and actions falling away. . . .

Meditate on God's Word. Read through the book of Psalms and see how many times David speaks of meditating on God's Word.

In Psalm 1 we read, "Blessed is the man who does not walk in the counsel of the wicked or stand in the way of sinners or sit in the seat of mockers." In other words, that person doesn't get his input from the wrong sources. "But his delight is in the law of the LORD [the Bible], and on his law he *meditates* day and night." As a result, "He is like a tree planted by streams of water, which yields its *fruit* in season and whose leaf does not wither. Whatever he does prospers" (emphasis added).

God says that when we meditate on his Word day and night, we will bear fruit. We will be fruitful, productive people—people full of love, joy, peace, patience, and the rest of the fruit of the Spirit. He also says we will prosper.

—God's Power to Change Your Life[1]

Then Jesus said to those Jews

who believed Him, "If you

abide in My word, you are

My disciples indeed. And you

shall know the truth, and the

truth shall make you free."

JOHN 8:31–32

GOD PROMISES A PLAN FOR YOUR LIFE

For we are His workmanship, created in Christ Jesus for good works, which God prepared beforehand that we should walk in them.

EPHESIANS 2:10

Then the word of the Lord came to me, saying:
"Before I formed you in the womb I knew you;
Before you were born I sanctified you.

JEREMIAH 1:4–5

Whatever you do, do it heartily, as to the Lord and not to men, knowing that from the Lord you will receive the reward of the inheritance; for you serve the Lord Christ.

COLOSSIANS 3:23–24

In their hearts humans plan their course,
but the Lord establishes their steps.

PROVERBS 16:9 NIV

Trust in the LORD, and do good;
Dwell in the land, and feed on His faithfulness.
Delight yourself also in the LORD,
And He shall give you the desires of your heart.

Commit your way to the LORD,
Trust also in Him,
And He shall bring it to pass.
He shall bring forth your righteousness as the light,
And your justice as the noonday.

PSALM 37:3–6

Blessed are those who keep my ways.
Hear instruction and be wise,
And do not disdain it.
Blessed is the man who listens to me,
Watching daily at my gates,
Waiting at the posts of my doors.
For whoever finds me finds life,
And obtains favor from the LORD.

PROVERBS 8:32–35

Serve the LORD with gladness;
Come before His presence with singing.
Know that the LORD, He is God;
It is He who has made us, and not we ourselves;
We are His people and the sheep of His pasture.

Enter into His gates with thanksgiving,
And into His courts with praise.
Be thankful to Him, and bless His name.
For the LORD is good;
His mercy is everlasting,
And His truth endures to all generations.

PSALM 100:2–5

Then Job answered the LORD and said:
"I know that You can do everything,
And that no purpose of Yours can be withheld from You."

JOB 42:1–2

Many, O LORD my God, are Your wonderful works
Which You have done;
And Your thoughts toward us
Cannot be recounted to You in order;
If I would declare and speak of them,
They are more than can be numbered.

PSALM 40:5

GOD PROMISES ANSWERED PRAYER

"Ask, and it will be given to you; seek, and you will find; knock, and it will be opened to you. For everyone who asks receives, and he who seeks finds, and to him who knocks it will be opened."

MATTHEW 7:7–8

"If you have faith and do not doubt, you will not only do what was done to the fig tree, but also if you say to this mountain, 'Be removed and be cast into the sea,' it will be done. And whatever things you ask in prayer, believing, you will receive."

MATTHEW 21:21–22

"If two of you agree on earth concerning anything that they ask, it will be done for them by My Father in heaven. For where two or three are gathered together in My name, I am there in the midst of them."

MATTHEW 18:19–20

"Therefore I say to you, whatever things you ask when you pray, believe that you receive them, and you will have them."

MARK 11:24

"I say to you, he who believes in Me, the works that I do he will do also; and greater works than these he will do, because I go to My Father. And whatever you ask in My name, that I will do, that the Father may be glorified in the Son. If you ask anything in My name, I will do it."

"Whatever you ask the Father in My name He will give you. Until now you have asked nothing in My name. Ask, and you will receive, that your joy may be full."

JOHN 16:23–24

The LORD is near to all who call upon Him,
To all who call upon Him in truth.
He will fulfill the desire of those who fear Him;
He also will hear their cry and save them.

PSALM 145:18–19

"When you pray, you shall not be like the hypocrites. For they love to pray standing in the synagogues and on the corners of the streets, that they may be seen by men. Assuredly, I say to you, they have their reward. But you, when you pray, go into your room, and when you have shut your door, pray to your Father who is in the secret place; and your Father who sees in secret will reward you openly."

MATTHEW 6:5–6

GOD PROMISES THE POWER OF HIS WORD

The law of the LORD is perfect, converting the soul;
The testimony of the LORD is sure, making wise the
    simple;
The statutes of the LORD are right, rejoicing the heart;
The commandment of the LORD is pure, enlightening
    the eyes;
The fear of the LORD is clean, enduring forever;
The judgments of the LORD are true and righteous
    altogether.
More to be desired are they than gold,
Yea, than much fine gold;
Sweeter also than honey and the honeycomb.
Moreover by them Your servant is warned,
And in keeping them there is great reward.

PSALM 19:7–11

Let the words of my mouth and the meditation of my
    heart
Be acceptable in Your sight,
O LORD, my strength and my Redeemer.

PSALM 19:14

"I have not spoken on My own authority; but the Father who sent Me gave Me a command, what I should say and what I should speak. And I know that His command is everlasting life. Therefore, whatever I speak, just as the Father has told Me, so I speak."

JOHN 12:49–50

All Scripture is given by inspiration of God, and is profitable for doctrine, for reproof, for correction, for instruction in righteousness, that the man of God may be complete, thoroughly equipped for every good work.

2 TIMOTHY 3:16–17

Your word is a lamp to my feet
And a light to my path.

PSALM 119:105

"So shall My word be that goes forth from My mouth;
It shall not return to Me void,
But it shall accomplish what I please,
And it shall prosper in the thing for which I sent it."

ISAIAH 55:11

Teach me, O LORD, the way of Your statutes,
And I shall keep it to the end.
Give me understanding, and I shall keep Your law;
Indeed, I shall observe it with my whole heart.
Make me walk in the path of Your commandments,
For I delight in it.

PSALM 119:33–35

For the word of God is living and powerful, and sharper than any two-edged sword, piercing even to the division of soul and spirit, and of joints and marrow, and is a discerner of the thoughts and intents of the heart.

HEBREWS 4:12

Every word of God has been proven true. He is a safe-covering to those who trust in Him.

PROVERBS 30:5 NLV

How can a young person stay on the path of purity?
By living according to your word.
I seek you with all my heart;
do not let me stray from your commands.

PSALM 119:9–10 NIV

GOD PROMISES HIS WILL FOR YOUR LIFE

Your ears shall hear a word behind you, saying,
"This is the way, walk in it,"
Whenever you turn to the right hand
Or whenever you turn to the left.

ISAIAH 30:21

If any of you lacks wisdom, let him ask of God, who gives to all liberally and without reproach, and it will be given to him. But let him ask in faith, with no doubting, for he who doubts is like a wave of the sea driven and tossed by the wind.

JAMES 1:5–6

When you roam, [God's commands] will lead you;
When you sleep, they will keep you;
And when you awake, they will speak with you.

PROVERBS 6:22

This Book of the Law shall not depart from your mouth, but you shall meditate in it day and night, that you may observe to do according to all that is written in it. For then you will make your way prosperous, and then you will have good success.

JOSHUA 1:8

For this is God,
Our God forever and ever;
He will be our guide
Even to death.

PSALM 48:14

All the ways of a man are pure in his own eyes,
But the LORD weighs the spirits.

Commit your works to the LORD,
And your thoughts will be established.

PROVERBS 16:2–3

The steps of a good man are ordered by the LORD,
And He delights in his way.

PSALM 37:23

Now may the God of peace who brought up our Lord Jesus from the dead, that great Shepherd of the sheep, through the blood of the everlasting covenant, make you complete in every good work to do His will, working in you what is well pleasing in His sight, through Jesus Christ, to whom be glory forever and ever. Amen.

HEBREWS 13:20–21

GOD PROMISES HIS WORD IS INFALLIBLE

By faith we understand that the worlds were framed by the word of God, so that the things which are seen were not made of things which are visible.

HEBREWS 11:3

In the beginning was the Word, and the Word was with God, and the Word was God. He was in the beginning with God. All things were made through Him, and without Him nothing was made that was made. In Him was life, and the life was the light of men. And the light shines in the darkness, and the darkness did not comprehend it. . . .

And the Word became flesh and dwelt among us, and we beheld His glory, the glory as of the only begotten of the Father, full of grace and truth.

JOHN 1:1–5, 14

"They are not of the world, just as I am not of the world. Sanctify them by Your truth. Your word is truth."

JOHN 17:16–17

Forever, O LORD,
Your word is settled in heaven.
Your faithfulness endures to all generations;
You established the earth, and it abides. . . .
Your word is a lamp to my feet
And a light to my path.
I have sworn and confirmed
That I will keep Your righteous judgments. . . .
Your testimonies are wonderful;
Therefore my soul keeps them.
The entrance of Your words gives light;
It gives understanding to the simple.

PSALM 119:89–90, 105–106, 129–130

I will praise You with my whole heart;
Before the gods I will sing praises to You.
I will worship toward Your holy temple,
And praise Your name
For Your lovingkindness and Your truth;
For You have magnified Your word above all Your name.

PSALM 138:1–2

So then faith comes by hearing, and hearing by the word
of God.

ROMANS 10:17

Your word is very pure;
Therefore Your servant loves it. . . .
My eyes are awake through the night watches,
That I may meditate on Your word.

PSALM 119:140, 148

Therefore lay aside all filthiness and overflow of wickedness, and receive with meekness the implanted word, which is able to save your souls. But be doers of the word, and not hearers only, deceiving yourselves.

JAMES 1:21–22

He who despises the word will be destroyed,
But he who fears the commandment will be rewarded.
The law of the wise is a fountain of life,
To turn one away from the snares of death.

PROVERBS 13:13–14

The entirety of Your word is truth,
And every one of Your righteous
judgments endures forever.

PSALM 119:160

GOD'S PROMISES IN ACTION

Which Bible promises from this section do you want to commit to memory?

....

....

....

....

What are you struggling with right now that the power of God's Word can help you overcome, change, or move beyond?

....

....

....

....

How can God's Word help you deepen your relationship with God?

....

....

....

....

ABIDING WITH THE FATHER, SON, AND HOLY SPIRIT

MAX LUCADO ON ABIDING IN CHRIST'S LOVE

Don't you need a fountain of love that won't run dry? You'll find one on a stone-cropped hill outside Jerusalem's walls where Jesus hangs, cross nailed and thorn crowned. . . . Remember this: "God showed his great love for us by sending Christ to die for us while we were still sinners" (Romans 5:8 NLT).

Don't trust other yardsticks. We often do. The sight of the healthy or successful prompts us to conclude, God must really love him. . . . Or we gravitate to the other extreme. Lonely and frail in the hospital bed, we deduce, God does not love me. How could he? Look at me.

Rebuff such thoughts! Success signals God's love no more than struggles indicate the lack of it. The definitive, God-sanctioned gauge is not a good day or a bad break but the dying hours of his Son. Consider them often. Let the gap between trips to the cross diminish daily. . . . Accept this invitation of Jesus: "Abide in My love" (John 15:9 NASB). . . .

To abide in Christ's love is to make his love your home. Not a roadside park or hotel room you occasionally visit, but your preferred dwelling. You rest in him. Eat in him. When thunder claps, you step beneath his roof. His walls secure you from the winds.

—Begin Again[2]

God is love. When we take up permanent residence in a life of love, we live in God and God lives in us. This way, love has the run of the house, becomes at home and mature in us, so that we're free of worry on Judgment Day—our standing in the world is identical with Christ's. There is no room in love for fear. Well-formed love banishes fear. Since fear is crippling, a fearful life—fear of death, fear of judgment— is one not yet fully formed in love.

1 JOHN 4:17–18 MSG

GOD PROMISES TO BE YOUR LOVING FATHER

For us there is one God, the Father, of whom are all things, and we for Him; and one Lord Jesus Christ, through whom are all things, and through whom we live.

1 CORINTHIANS 8:6

A father of the fatherless, a defender of widows,
Is God in His holy habitation.

PSALM 68:5

But now, O Lord,
You are our Father;
We are the clay, and You our potter;
And all we are the work of Your hand.

ISAIAH 64:8

Every good gift and every perfect gift is from above, and comes down from the Father of lights, with whom there is no variation or shadow of turning.

JAMES 1:17

Behold what manner of love the Father has bestowed on us, that we should be called children of God!

1 JOHN 3:1

"As the Father loved Me, I also have loved you; abide in My love. If you keep My commandments, you will abide in My love, just as I have kept My Father's commandments and abide in His love."

JOHN 15:9–10

The Lord has appeared of old to me, saying:
"Yes, I have loved you with an everlasting love;
Therefore with lovingkindness I have drawn you."

JEREMIAH 31:3

I am persuaded that neither death nor life, nor angels nor principalities nor powers, nor things present nor things to come, nor height nor depth, nor any other created thing, shall be able to separate us from the love of God which is in Christ Jesus our Lord.

ROMANS 8:38–39

"Beloved, let us love one another, for love is of God; and everyone who loves is born of God and knows God. He who does not love does not know God, for God is love.

1 JOHN 4:7–8

GOD PROMISES YOU HIS SON, YOUR SAVIOR

He has delivered us from the power of darkness and conveyed us into the kingdom of the Son of His love, in whom we have redemption through His blood, the forgiveness of sins.

He is the image of the invisible God, the firstborn over all creation. For by Him all things were created that are in heaven and that are on earth, visible and invisible, whether thrones or dominions or principalities or powers. All things were created through Him and for Him. And He is before all things, and in Him all things consist. And He is the head of the body, the church, who is the beginning, the firstborn from the dead, that in all things He may have the preeminence.

For it pleased the Father that in Him all the fullness should dwell, and by Him to reconcile all things to Himself, by Him, whether things on earth or things in heaven, having made peace through the blood of His cross.

COLOSSIANS 1:13–20

And my spirit has rejoiced in God my Savior. . . .
For He who is mighty has done great things for me,
And holy is His name.
And His mercy is on those who fear Him
From generation to generation.

LUKE 1:47, 49–50

God, who at various times and in various ways spoke in time past to the fathers by the prophets, has in these last days spoken to us by His Son, whom He has appointed heir of all things, through whom also He made the worlds; who being the brightness of His glory and the express image of His person, and upholding all things by the word of His power, when He had by Himself purged our sins, sat down at the right hand of the Majesty on high, having become so much better than the angels, as He has by inheritance obtained a more excellent name than they.

HEBREWS 1:1–4

And truly Jesus did many other signs in the presence of His disciples, which are not written in this book; but these are written that you may believe that Jesus is the Christ, the Son of God, and that believing you may have life in His name.

JOHN 20:30–31

For God so loved the world that He gave His only begotten Son, that whoever believes in Him should not perish but have everlasting life.

JOHN 3:16

For I have come down from heaven, not to do My own will, but the will of Him who sent Me.

JOHN 6:38

GOD PROMISES YOU THE GIFT OF THE HOLY SPIRIT, YOUR COMFORTER

"The Helper, the Holy Spirit, whom the Father will send in My name, He will teach you all things, and bring to your remembrance all things that I said to you."

JOHN 14:26

Do you not know that your body is the temple of the Holy Spirit who is in you, whom you have from God, and you are not your own? For you were bought at a price; therefore glorify God in your body and in your spirit, which are God's.

1 CORINTHIANS 6:19–20

"It shall come to pass afterward
That I will pour out My Spirit on all flesh."

JOEL 2:28

"I will pray the Father, and He will give you another Helper, that He may abide with you forever—the Spirit of truth, whom the world cannot receive, because it neither sees Him nor knows Him; but you know Him, for He dwells with you and will be in you."

JOHN 14:16–17

"When He, the Spirit of truth, has come, He will guide you into all truth; for He will not speak on His own authority, but whatever He hears He will speak; and He will tell you things to come. He will glorify Me, for He will take of what is Mine and declare it to you."

JOHN 16:13–14

Being assembled together with [the apostles He had chosen], [Jesus] commanded them not to depart from Jerusalem, but to wait for the Promise of the Father, "which," He said, "you have heard from Me; for John truly baptized with water, but you shall be baptized with the Holy Spirit not many days from now. . . . You shall receive power when the Holy Spirit has come upon you; and you shall be witnesses to Me in Jerusalem, and in all Judea and Samaria, and to the end of the earth."

ACTS 1:4–5, 8

I indeed baptize you with water unto repentance, but He who is coming after me is mightier than I, whose sandals I am not worthy to carry. He will baptize you with the Holy Spirit and fire.

MATTHEW 3:11

GOD PROMISES YOU HIS COVENANT

Therefore remember that you, once Gentiles in the flesh—who are called Uncircumcision by what is called the Circumcision made in the flesh by hands—that at that time you were without Christ, being aliens from the commonwealth of Israel and strangers from the covenants of promise, having no hope and without God in the world. But now in Christ Jesus you who once were far off have been brought near by the blood of Christ.

For He Himself is our peace, who has made both one, and has broken down the middle wall of separation, having abolished in His flesh the enmity, that is, the law of commandments contained in ordinances, so as to create in Himself one new man from the two, thus making peace.

EPHESIANS 2:11–15

But now He has obtained a more excellent ministry, inasmuch as He is also Mediator of a better covenant, which was established on better promises.

For if that first covenant had been faultless, then no place would have been sought for a second. Because finding fault with them, He says: "Behold, the days are coming, says the LORD, when I will make a new covenant with the house of Israel and with the house of Judah—not according to the covenant that I made with their fathers in the day when I took them by the hand to lead them out of the land of Egypt; because they did not continue in My covenant, and I disregarded them, says the LORD. For this is the covenant that I will make with the house of Israel after those days, says the LORD: I will put My laws in their mind and write them on their hearts; and I will be their God, and they shall be My people. None of them shall teach his neighbor, and none his brother, saying, 'Know the LORD,' for all shall know Me, from the least of them to the greatest of them. For I will be merciful to their unrighteousness, and their sins and their lawless deeds I will remember no more."

In that He says, "A new covenant," He has made the first obsolete. Now what is becoming obsolete and growing old is ready to vanish away.

HEBREWS 8:6–13

Brethren, I speak in the manner of men: Though it is only a man's covenant, yet if it is confirmed, no one annuls or adds to it. Now to Abraham and his Seed were the promises made. He does not say, "And to seeds," as of many, but as of one, "And to your Seed," who is Christ. And this I say, that the law, which was four hundred and thirty years later, cannot annul the covenant that was confirmed before by God in Christ, that it should make the promise of no effect. For if the inheritance is of the law, it is no longer of promise; but God gave it to Abraham by promise.

What purpose then does the law serve? It was added because of transgressions, till the Seed should come to whom the promise was made; and it was appointed through angels by the hand of a mediator. Now a mediator does not mediate for one only, but God is one.

Is the law then against the promises of God? Certainly not! For if there had been a law given which could have given life, truly righteousness would have been by the law. But the Scripture has confined all under sin, that the promise by faith in Jesus Christ might be given to those who believe.

But before faith came, we were kept under guard by the law, kept for the faith which would afterward be revealed. Therefore the law was our tutor to bring us to Christ, that we might be justified by faith. But after faith has come, we are no longer under a tutor.

For you are all sons of God through faith in Christ Jesus. For as many of you as were baptized into Christ have put on Christ. There is neither Jew nor Greek, there is neither slave nor free, there is neither male nor female; for you are all one in Christ Jesus. And if you are Christ's, then you are Abraham's seed, and heirs according to the promise.

GALATIANS 3:15–29

For when God made a promise to Abraham, because He could swear by no one greater, He swore by Himself, saying, "Surely blessing I will bless you, and multiplying I will multiply you." And so, after he had patiently endured, he obtained the promise.

For men indeed swear by the greater, and an oath for

confirmation is for them an end of all dispute. Thus God, determining to show more abundantly to the heirs of promise the immutability of His counsel, confirmed it by an oath, that by two immutable things, in which it is impossible for God to lie, we might have strong consolation, who have fled for refuge to lay hold of the hope set before us. This hope we have as an anchor of the soul, both sure and steadfast, and which enters the Presence behind the veil.

HEBREWS 6:13–19

Who is the man that fears the LORD?
Him shall He teach in the way He chooses.
He himself shall dwell in prosperity,
And his descendants shall inherit the earth.
The secret of the LORD is with those who fear Him,
And He will show them His covenant.

PSALM 25:12–14

How much more shall the blood of Christ, who through the eternal Spirit offered Himself without spot to God, cleanse your conscience from dead works to serve the living God?

And for this reason He is the Mediator of the new covenant, by means of death, for the redemption of the transgressions under the first covenant, that those who are called may receive the promise of the eternal inheritance.

HEBREWS 9:14–15

"Behold, the days are coming, says the LORD, when I will make a new covenant with the house of Israel and with the house of Judah—not according to the covenant that I made with their fathers in the day that I took them by the hand to lead them out of the land of Egypt, My covenant which they broke, though I was a husband to them, says the LORD. But this is the covenant that I will make with the house of Israel after those days, says the LORD: I will put My law in their minds, and write it on their hearts; and I will be their God, and they shall be My people."

JEREMIAH 31:31–33

And we have such trust through Christ toward God. Not that we are sufficient of ourselves to think of anything as being from ourselves, but our sufficiency is from God, who also made us sufficient as ministers of the new covenant, not of the letter but of the Spirit; for the letter kills, but the Spirit gives life.

2 CORINTHIANS 3:4–6

Likewise He also took the cup after supper, saying, "This cup is the new covenant in My blood, which is shed for you."

LUKE 22:20

GOD PROMISES YOU HIS PLAN OF SALVATION

Therefore, just as through one man sin entered the world, and death through sin, and thus death spread to all men, because all sinned.

ROMANS 5:12

God wants everyone to be saved and to know the whole truth.

1 TIMOTHY 2:4 CEV

For the wages of sin is death, but the gift of God is eternal life in Christ Jesus our Lord.

ROMANS 6:23

But God demonstrates His own love toward us, in that while we were still sinners, Christ died for us.

ROMANS 5:8

All that the Father gives Me will come to Me, and the one who comes to Me I will by no means cast out.

JOHN 6:37

Moreover, brethren, I declare to you the gospel which I preached to you, which also you received and in which you stand, by which also you are saved, if you hold fast that word which I preached to you—unless you believed in vain. For I delivered to you first of all that which I also received: that Christ died for our sins according to the Scriptures, and that He was buried, and that He rose again the third day according to the Scriptures.

1 CORINTHIANS 15:1–4

For I am not ashamed of the gospel of Christ, for it is the power of God to salvation for everyone who believes, for the Jew first and also for the Greek.

ROMANS 1:16

"He who believes in the Son has everlasting life; and he who does not believe the Son shall not see life, but the wrath of God abides on him."

JOHN 3:36

But as many as received Him, to them He gave the right to become children of God, to those who believe in His name.

JOHN 1:12

GOD'S PROMISES IN ACTION

Which Bible promises from this section do you want to commit to memory?

....

....

....

....

What are you struggling with right now that you need to take to God in prayer?

....

....

....

....

How can you deepen your relationship with God through prayer?

....

....

....

....

YOUR FAITH JOURNEY

CRAIG GROESCHEL ON MATURITY AND YOUR PRAYER LIFE

I was struck by the simplicity of [Jabez's prayer in 1 Chronicles 4]: Bless me. Enlarge my territory. Let your hand be with me. Keep me from harm so that I will be free from pain. . . .

Keep me from harm and free from pain makes sense. Who wants hardship? Who wants to struggle? But I wonder if we might as well be praying, "God, don't let me grow. Don't let me get stronger. Don't allow me to trust you more." Even though trials are never fun or easy to endure, God can often use them for his purposes. In fact, James . . . was bold enough to tell us we should be thankful for the way God uses hardship to perfect us: "Consider it pure joy, my brothers and sisters, whenever you face trials of many kinds, because you know that the testing of your faith produces perseverance. Let perseverance finish its work so that you may be mature and complete, not lacking anything" (James 1:2–4 NIV).

If we pray only for protection from trials, then we rob ourselves of our future maturity. . . . But if that's our only desire, our biggest priority, then we may miss the perseverance that our trials produce. . . .

Instead of just asking God to keep you safe, give you more, and protect your life, you may have to ask God to break you.

—*Dangerous Prayers*[3]

Now Jabez was more honorable than his brothers, and his mother called his name Jabez, saying, "Because I bore him in pain." And Jabez called on the God of Israel saying, "Oh, that You would bless me indeed, and enlarge my territory, that Your hand would be with me, and that You would keep me from evil, that I may not cause pain!" So God granted him what he requested.

1 CHRONICLES 4:9–10

GOD PROMISES YOU HELP WHEN
WAITING IS DIFFICULT

My soul, wait silently for God alone,
For my expectation is from Him.
He only is my rock and my salvation;
He is my defense;
I shall not be moved.
In God is my salvation and my glory;
The rock of my strength,
And my refuge, is in God.

PSALM 62:5-7

Our soul waits for the LORD;
He is our help and our shield.
For our heart shall rejoice in Him,
Because we have trusted in His holy name.
Let Your mercy, O LORD, be upon us,
Just as we hope in You.

PSALM 33:20-22

Those who wait on the LORD
Shall renew their strength;
They shall mount up with wings like eagles,
They shall run and not be weary,
They shall walk and not faint.

ISAIAH 40:31

I wait for the LORD, my soul waits,
And in His word I do hope.
My soul waits for the Lord
More than those who watch for the morning—
Yes, more than those who watch for the morning.

PSALM 130:5–6

Wait on the LORD;
Be of good courage,
And He shall strengthen your heart;
Wait, I say, on the LORD!

PSALM 27:14

We have become partakers of Christ if we hold the beginning
of our confidence steadfast to the end.

HEBREWS 3:14

It will be said in that day:
"Behold, this is our God;
We have waited for Him, and He will save us.
This is the LORD;
We have waited for Him;
We will be glad and rejoice in His salvation."

ISAIAH 25:9

I waited patiently for the LORD;
And He inclined to me,
And heard my cry.
He also brought me up out of a horrible pit,
Out of the miry clay,
And set my feet upon a rock,
And established my steps.
He has put a new song in my mouth—
Praise to our God;
Many will see it and fear,
And will trust in the LORD.

PSALM 40:1–3

For the LORD is a God of justice;
Blessed are all those who wait for Him.

ISAIAH 30:18

GOD PROMISES YOU HELP THROUGH CHRISTIAN FELLOWSHIP

Let us consider one another in order to stir up love and good works, not forsaking the assembling of ourselves together, as is the manner of some, but exhorting one another, and so much the more as you see the Day approaching.

HEBREWS 10:24–25

Whoever has this world's goods, and sees his brother in need, and shuts up his heart from him, how does the love of God abide in him? My little children, let us not love in word or in tongue, but in deed and in truth.

1 JOHN 3:17–18

Let the word of Christ dwell in you richly in all wisdom, teaching and admonishing one another in psalms and hymns and spiritual songs, singing with grace in your hearts to the Lord.

COLOSSIANS 3:16

Walk in love, as Christ also has loved us and given Himself for us, an offering and a sacrifice to God for a sweet-smelling aroma. . . . Speaking to one another in psalms and hymns and spiritual songs, singing and making melody in your heart to the Lord. . . . For we are members of His body, of His flesh and of His bones.

EPHESIANS 5:2, 19, 30

"I am no longer in the world, but these are in the world, and I come to You. Holy Father, keep through Your name those whom You have given Me, that they may be one as We are. . . . [May] they all may be one, as You, Father, are in Me, and I in You; that they also may be one in Us, that the world may believe that You sent Me. And the glory which You gave Me I have given them, that they may be one just as We are one: I in them, and You in Me; that they may be made perfect in one, and that the world may know that You have sent Me, and have loved them as You have loved Me."

JOHN 17:11, 21–23

Two people are better off than one, for they can help each other succeed.

ECCLESIASTES 4:9 NLT

[New believers] continued steadfastly in the apostles' doctrine and fellowship, in the breaking of bread, and in prayers. . . . So continuing daily with one accord in the temple, and breaking bread from house to house, they ate their food with gladness and simplicity of heart, praising God and having favor with all the people. And the Lord added to the church daily those who were being saved.

ACTS 2:42, 46–47

May the God of patience and comfort grant you to be like-minded toward one another, according to Christ Jesus, that you may with one mind and one mouth glorify the God and Father of our Lord Jesus Christ.

ROMANS 15:5–7

Therefore encourage one another and build each other up, just as in fact you are doing.

1 THESSALONIANS 5:11 NIV

A person standing alone can be attacked and defeated, but two can stand back-to-back and conquer. Three are even better, for a triple-braided cord is not easily broken.

ECCLESIASTES 4:12 NLT

GOD PROMISES YOU THE GIFT OF HIS GRACE

The LORD God is a sun and shield;
The LORD will give grace and glory;
No good thing will He withhold
From those who walk uprightly.

O LORD of hosts,
Blessed is the man who trusts in You!

PSALM 84:11–12

He who raised up the Lord Jesus will also raise us up with
Jesus, and will present us with you. For all things are for your
sakes, that grace, having spread through the many, may cause
thanksgiving to abound to the glory of God.

2 CORINTHIANS 4:14–15

He who loves purity of heart
And has grace on his lips,
The king will be his friend.

PROVERBS 22:11

Blessed be the God and Father of our Lord Jesus Christ, who has blessed us with every spiritual blessing in the heavenly places in Christ, just as He chose us in Him before the foundation of the world, that we should be holy and without blame before Him in love, having predestined us to adoption as sons by Jesus Christ to Himself, according to the good pleasure of His will, to the praise of the glory of His grace, by which He made us accepted in the Beloved.

EPHESIANS 1:3–6

All have sinned and fall short of the glory of God, being justified freely by His grace through the redemption that is in Christ Jesus, whom God set forth as a propitiation by His blood, through faith, to demonstrate His righteousness, because in His forbearance God had passed over the sins that were previously committed, to demonstrate at the present time His righteousness, that He might be just and the justifier of the one who has faith in Jesus.

ROMANS 3:23–26

By grace you have been saved through faith, and that not of yourselves; it is the gift of God, not of works, lest anyone should boast.

EPHESIANS 2:8–9

The law was given through Moses, but grace and truth came through Jesus Christ.

JOHN 1:17

The free gift [of forgiveness and eternal life] is not like the offense. For if by the one man's offense many died, much more the grace of God and the gift by the grace of the one Man, Jesus Christ, abounded to many. . . . For if by the one man's offense death reigned through the one, much more those who receive abundance of grace and of the gift of righteousness will reign in life through the One, Jesus Christ.

ROMANS 5:15, 17

For the grace of God that brings salvation has appeared to all men, teaching us that, denying ungodliness and worldly lusts, we should live soberly, righteously, and godly in the present age, looking for the blessed hope and glorious appearing of our great God and Savior Jesus Christ, who gave Himself for us, that He might redeem us from every lawless deed and purify for Himself His own special people, zealous for good works.

TITUS 2:11–14

GOD PROMISES YOU THE GIFT OF EFFECTIVE PRAYER

Be anxious for nothing, but in everything by prayer and supplication, with thanksgiving, let your requests be made known to God; and the peace of God, which surpasses all understanding, will guard your hearts and minds through Christ Jesus.

PHILIPPIANS 4:6–7

"Call to Me, and I will answer you, and show you great and mighty things, which you do not know."

JEREMIAH 33:3

"So I say to you, ask, and it will be given to you; seek, and you will find; knock, and it will be opened to you."

LUKE 11:9

"Assuredly, I say to you, whatever you bind on earth will be bound in heaven, and whatever you loose on earth will be loosed in heaven. Again I say to you that if two of you agree on earth concerning anything that they ask, it will be done for them by My Father in heaven."

MATTHEW 18:18–19

Confess your trespasses to one another, and pray for one another, that you may be healed. The effective, fervent prayer of a righteous man avails much. Elijah was a man with a nature like ours, and he prayed earnestly that it would not rain; and it did not rain on the land for three years and six months. And he prayed again, and the heaven gave rain, and the earth produced its fruit.

JAMES 5:16–18

If we confess our sins, He is faithful and just to forgive us our sins and to cleanse us from all unrighteousness.

1 JOHN 1:9

"And when you pray, you shall not be like the hypocrites. For they love to pray standing in the synagogues and on the corners of the streets, that they may be seen by men. Assuredly, I say to you, they have their reward. But you, when you pray, go into your room, and when you have shut your door, pray to your Father who is in the secret place; and your Father who sees in secret will reward you openly."

MATTHEW 6:5–6

GOD PROMISES THE GIFT OF SPIRITUAL GROWTH

Add to your faith virtue, to virtue knowledge, to knowledge self-control, to self-control perseverance, to perseverance godliness, to godliness brotherly kindness, and to brotherly kindness love. For if these things are yours and abound, you will be neither barren nor unfruitful in the knowledge of our Lord Jesus Christ.

2 PETER 1:5–8

Grow in the grace and knowledge of our Lord and Savior Jesus Christ. To Him be the glory both now and forever. Amen.

2 PETER 3:18

As newborn babes, desire the pure milk of the word, that you may grow thereby, if indeed you have tasted that the Lord is gracious.

1 PETER 2:2–3

Be an example to the believers in word, in conduct, in love, in spirit, in faith, in purity. . . . Meditate on these things; give yourself entirely to them, that your progress may be evident to all. Take heed to yourself and to the doctrine. Continue in them, for in doing this you will save both yourself and those who hear you.

1 TIMOTHY 4:12, 15–16

I bow my knees to the Father of our Lord Jesus Christ, from whom the whole family in heaven and earth is named, that He would grant you, according to the riches of His glory, to be strengthened with might through His Spirit in the inner man, that Christ may dwell in your hearts through faith; that you, being rooted and grounded in love, may be able to comprehend with all the saints what is the width and length and depth and height—to know the love of Christ which passes knowledge; that you may be filled with all the fullness of God.

EPHESIANS 3:14–19

Be diligent to present yourself approved to God, a worker who does not need to be ashamed, rightly dividing the word of truth.

2 TIMOTHY 2:15

The Lord is the Spirit; and where the Spirit of the Lord is, there is liberty. But we all, with unveiled face, beholding as in a mirror the glory of the Lord, are being transformed into the same image from glory to glory, just as by the Spirit of the Lord.

2 CORINTHIANS 3:17–18

GOD'S PROMISES IN ACTION

Which Bible promises from this section do you want to
commit to memory?

....

....

....

....

What are you struggling with right now in your faith journey?

....

....

....

....

What are some ways you can deepen your faith journey with
God and with the fellow members of your faith community?

....

....

....

....

GOD'S PROMISES
FOR DEALING WITH
YOUR EMOTIONS

DAVID JEREMIAH ON LIBERATION FROM LONELINESS

When something is broken we consult the original manufacturer, and for human beings God is the Original Manufacturer. He created us with certain attributes, and one of them is that we have an emptiness only He can fill. . . . Nothing in this world will ultimately satisfy us short of knowing the One who made us. So the most basic loneliness of humanity is the loneliness of estrangement from God. It has no remedy but one. . . .

I've been a people-watcher. I can tell if you are a believer or not simply by observing how you handle your problems. If you lack the inner strength of a godly man or woman, you'll finally buckle under the stress, the strife, and the struggles. You will lack the most basic resource for dealing with the most basic problem. But if you know Him, here's what happens: You're connected to Someone who came into the world, hung on a cross, and experienced ultimate loneliness so you would never have to do so. . . .

Now you and I walk in the light. We can know God intimately as His beloved children. It's possible to know liberation from loneliness in the warmth of His love. It happens as we embrace His lordship over us and He takes residence within us. He fills that void, and we begin to know peace and fulfillment and abundance.

—Slaying the Giants in Your Life[4]

Turn to me and be gracious to me,

for I am lonely and afflicted.

Relieve the troubles of my heart

and free me from my anguish.

PSALM 25:16–17 NIV

GOD PROMISES TO MEET YOU WHEN
YOU FEEL DISCOURAGED

Then Jesus said to them again, "Most assuredly, I say to you, I am the door of the sheep. All who ever came before Me are thieves and robbers, but the sheep did not hear them. I am the door. If anyone enters by Me, he will be saved, and will go in and out and find pasture. The thief does not come except to steal, and to kill, and to destroy. I have come that they may have life, and that they may have it more abundantly.

"I am the good shepherd. The good shepherd gives His life for the sheep."

JOHN 10:7–11

Though I walk in the midst of trouble, You will
    revive me;
You will stretch out Your hand
Against the wrath of my enemies,
And Your right hand will save me.
The LORD will perfect that which concerns me;
Your mercy, O LORD, endures forever;
Do not forsake the works of Your hands.

PSALM 138:7–8

"Let not your heart be troubled; you believe in God, believe also in Me. In My Father's house are many mansions; if it were not so, I would have told you. I go to prepare a place for you. And if I go and prepare a place for you, I will come again and receive you to Myself; that where I am, there you may be also."

JOHN 14:1–3

Let us run with endurance the race that is set before us, looking unto Jesus, the author and finisher of our faith.

HEBREWS 12:1–2

[Be] confident of this very thing, that He who has begun a good work in you will complete it until the day of Jesus Christ.

PHILIPPIANS 1:6

Love the LORD, all you godly ones!
    For the LORD protects those who are loyal to him,
    but he harshly punishes the arrogant.
So be strong and courageous,
    all you who put your hope in the LORD!

PSALM 31:23–24 NLT

GOD PROMISES TO MEET YOU
WHEN YOU FEEL LONELY

You will show me the way of life. Being with You is to be full of joy. In Your right hand there is happiness forever.

PSALM 16:11 NLV

God is our refuge and strength,
A very present help in trouble. . . .
The LORD of hosts is with us;
The God of Jacob is our refuge.

PSALM 46:1, 7

Turn to me and show me Your loving-kindness. For I am alone and in trouble.

PSALM 25:16 NLV

Draw near to God and He will draw near to you.

JAMES 4:8

The LORD your God, He is the One who goes with you. He will not leave you nor forsake you.

DEUTERONOMY 31:6

"For the mountains shall depart
And the hills be removed,
But My kindness shall not depart from you,
Nor shall My covenant of peace be removed,"
Says the Lord, who has mercy on you.

ISAIAH 54:10

There is no one like the God of Jeshurun,
Who rides the heavens to help you,
And in His excellency on the clouds.
The eternal God is your refuge,
And underneath are the everlasting arms.

DEUTERONOMY 33:26–27

[The Lord] heals the brokenhearted
And binds up their wounds.
He counts the number of the stars;
He calls them all by name.
Great is our Lord, and mighty in power;
His understanding is infinite.

PSALM 147:3–5

GOD PROMISES TO MEET YOU WHEN
YOU FEEL DEPRESSED

[The Lord's] favor is for life;
Weeping may endure for a night,
But joy comes in the morning.

PSALM 30:5

"If you love Me, keep My commandments. . . . I will not
leave you orphans; I will come to you. A little while longer and
the world will see Me no more, but you will see Me. Because I
live, you will live also."

JOHN 14:15, 18–19

The eyes of the Lord are on the righteous,
And His ears are open to their cry. . . .

The righteous cry out, and the Lord hears,
And delivers them out of all their troubles.
The Lord is near to those who have a broken heart,
And saves such as have a contrite spirit.

PSALM 34:15, 17–18

"And the LORD, He is the One who goes before you. He will be with you, He will not leave you nor forsake you; do not fear nor be dismayed."

DEUTERONOMY 31:8

When you pass through the waters, I will be with you;
And through the rivers, they shall not overflow you. . . .
For I am the LORD your God,
The Holy One of Israel, your Savior.

ISAIAH 43:2–3

Answer me speedily, O LORD;
My spirit fails!
Do not hide Your face from me,
Lest I be like those who go down into the pit.
Cause me to hear Your lovingkindness in the morning,
For in You do I trust;
Cause me to know the way in which I should walk,
For I lift up my soul to You.

PSALM 143:7–8

GOD PROMISES TO MEET YOU
WHEN YOU FEEL ANGRY

Let every man be swift to hear, slow to speak, slow to wrath; for the wrath of man does not produce the righteousness of God.

JAMES 1:19–20

Putting away lying, "Let each one of you speak truth with his neighbor," for we are members of one another. "Be angry, and do not sin": do not let the sun go down on your wrath, nor give place to the devil.

EPHESIANS 4:25–27

A soft answer turns away wrath,
But a harsh word stirs up anger.
The tongue of the wise uses knowledge rightly,
But the mouth of fools pours forth foolishness.

PROVERBS 15:1–2

He who is slow to wrath has great understanding,
But he who is impulsive exalts folly.

PROVERBS 14:29

He who is slow to anger is better than the mighty,
And he who rules his spirit than he who takes a city.

PROVERBS 16:32

If your enemy is hungry, give him bread to eat;
And if he is thirsty, give him water to drink;
For so you will heap coals of fire on his head,
And the LORD will reward you.

PROVERBS 25:21–22

Put off all these: anger, wrath, malice, blasphemy, filthy
language out of your mouth. Do not lie to one another, since
you have put off the old man with his deeds, and have put on the
new man who is renewed in knowledge according to the image of
Him who created him.

COLOSSIANS 3:8–10

Do not hasten in your spirit to be angry,
For anger rests in the bosom of fools.

ECCLESIASTES 7:9

A wise man fears and departs from evil,
But a fool rages and is self-confident.
A quick-tempered man acts foolishly,
And a man of wicked intentions is hated.

PROVERBS 14:16–17

GOD PROMISES TO MEET YOU
WHEN YOU FEEL CONFUSED

Trust in the LORD with all your heart,
And lean not on your own understanding;
In all your ways acknowledge Him,
And He shall direct your paths.

PROVERBS 3:5–6

The wisdom that is from above is first pure, then peaceable, gentle, willing to yield, full of mercy and good fruits, without partiality and without hypocrisy. Now the fruit of righteousness is sown in peace by those who make peace.

JAMES 3:17–18

Cast your burden on the LORD,
And He shall sustain you;
He shall never permit the righteous to be moved.

PSALM 55:22

"The Lord God will help Me;
Therefore I will not be disgraced;
Therefore I have set My face like a flint,
And I know that I will not be ashamed.
He is near who justifies Me;
Who will contend with Me?
Let us stand together.
Who is My adversary?
Let him come near Me. . . .

"Who among you fears the Lord?
Who obeys the voice of His Servant?
Who walks in darkness
And has no light?
Let him trust in the name of the Lord
And rely upon his God."

ISAIAH 50:7–8, 10

You are my hiding place;
You shall preserve me from trouble;
You shall surround me with songs of deliverance. *Selah*

I will instruct you and teach you in the way you
    should go;
I will guide you with My eye.

PSALM 32:7–8

But the Helper, the Holy Spirit, whom the Father will send in My name, He will teach you all things, and bring to your remembrance all things that I said to you.

JOHN 14:26

You were chosen through His loving-favor. But now you are turning and listening to another kind of good news. No! There is not another kind of good news. There are some who would like to lead you in the wrong way. They want to change the Good News about Christ. Even if we or an angel from heaven should preach another kind of good news to you that is not the one we preached, let him be cursed. As we said before, I will say it again. If any man is preaching another good news to you which is not the one you have received, let him be cursed.

GALATIANS 1:6–9 NLV

But the LORD is with me as a mighty, awesome One. Therefore my persecutors will stumble, and will not prevail.

JEREMIAH 20:11

GOD'S PROMISES IN ACTION

Which Bible promises from this section do you want to commit to memory?

....

....

....

....

What emotions are you struggling with right now that you need to bring before God?

....

....

....

....

When your emotions are getting the best of you, what are ways you can deepen your relationship with God?

....

....

....

....

GOD PROMISES TO HEAL
YOUR RELATIONSHIPS

SARAH JAKES ROBERTS ON FORGIVING YOURSELF

The deeper conversation you must be willing to have is how you forgive yourself.

You cannot punish yourself for relationships that did not live up to your expectations. I hope you forgive yourself for not loving yourself, for not thinking highly enough of yourself to demand the best from and for your heart. I hope you're pacified by the knowledge that you're not the only one who has ever made a choice that made them question themselves later, but I'm praying that you see there is still an opportunity for you to love yourself now. Love is so powerful that even from where you stand now you can learn to love the person you once were. You don't have to separate yourself any longer. You don't have to wish that you had chosen a different path. I can promise you that even in the midst of those moments that God was loving you, just as He is loving you now. You may ask yourself, How is this possible? It's because He created the blueprint for forgiveness. He knew that even as you were doing the very thing that hurt you, you were only doing so because you were seeking all of the components of love. The kind of love that 1 Corinthians 13 talks about.

—*Don't Settle for Safe*[5]

"So I tell you that all her sins are forgiven,

and that is why she has shown great love.

But anyone who has been forgiven for only

a little will show only a little love."

Then Jesus said to the woman,

"Your sins are forgiven."

Some other guests started saying to one another,

"Who is this who dares to forgive sins?"

But Jesus told the woman, "Because

of your faith, you are now saved. May

God give you peace!"

LUKE 7:47–50 CEV

GOD PROMISES TO HEAL YOUR

BROKEN RELATIONSHIPS

All of you be of one mind, having compassion for one another; love as brothers, be tenderhearted, be courteous; not returning evil for evil or reviling for reviling, but on the contrary blessing, knowing that you were called to this, that you may inherit a blessing. For

"He who would love life
And see good days,
Let him refrain his tongue from evil,
And his lips from speaking deceit.
Let him turn away from evil and do good;
Let him seek peace and pursue it."

1 PETER 3:8–11

A man shall leave his father and mother and be joined to his wife, and they shall become one flesh.

GENESIS 2:24

Wives, submit to your own husbands, as to the Lord. For the husband is head of the wife, as also Christ is head of the church; and He is the Savior of the body. Therefore, just as the church is subject to Christ, so let the wives be to their own husbands in everything.

Husbands, love your wives, just as Christ also loved the church and gave Himself for her, that He might sanctify and cleanse her with the washing of water by the word, that He might present her to Himself a glorious church, not having spot or wrinkle or any such thing, but that she should be holy and without blemish. So husbands ought to love their own wives as their own bodies; he who loves his wife loves himself. For no one ever hated his own flesh, but nourishes and cherishes it, just as the Lord does the church. For we are members of His body, of His flesh and of His bones.

EPHESIANS 5:22–30

Let all bitterness, wrath, anger, clamor, and evil speaking be put away from you, with all malice. And be kind to one another, tenderhearted, forgiving one another, even as God in Christ forgave you.

EPHESIANS 4:31–32

If it seems evil to you to serve the LORD, choose for your-selves this day whom you will serve, whether the gods which your fathers served that were on the other side of the River, or the gods of the Amorites, in whose land you dwell. But as for me and my house, we will serve the LORD.

JOSHUA 24:15

We have come to know and believe the love God has for us. God is love. If you live in love, you live by the help of God and God lives in you.

1 JOHN 4:16 NLV

You number my wanderings;
Put my tears into Your bottle;
Are they not in Your book?
When I cry out to You,
Then my enemies will turn back;
This I know, because God is for me.

PSALM 56:8–9

[Love] does not rejoice in iniquity, but rejoices in the truth; bears all things, believes all things, hopes all things, endures all things. . . . And now abide faith, hope, love, these three; but the greatest of these is love.

1 CORINTHIANS 13:6–7, 13

GOD PROMISES TO HEAL YOU WHEN
YOU FEEL ABANDONED

The Lord also will be a refuge for the oppressed,
A refuge in times of trouble.
And those who know Your name will put their trust
    in You;
For You, Lord, have not forsaken those who seek You.

PSALM 9:9–10

When you turn to the Lord your God and obey His voice
(for the Lord your God is a merciful God), He will not forsake
you nor destroy you, nor forget the covenant of your fathers
which He swore to them.

DEUTERONOMY 4:30–31

Hear, O Lord, when I cry with my voice! . . .
Do not hide Your face from me;
Do not turn Your servant away in anger;
You have been my help;
Do not leave me nor forsake me,
O God of my salvation.

PSALM 27:7, 9

Why are you cast down, O my soul?
And why are you disquieted within me?
Hope in God;
For I shall yet praise Him,
The help of my countenance and my God.

PSALM 43:5

The Lord will not forsake His people, for His great name's sake, because it has pleased the Lord to make you His people.

1 SAMUEL 12:22

"Because he has set his love upon Me, therefore I will
        deliver him;
I will set him on high, because he has known My name.
He shall call upon Me, and I will answer him;
I will be with him in trouble;
I will deliver him and honor him."

PSALM 91:14–15

"Can a woman forget her nursing child,
And not have compassion on the son of her womb?
Surely they may forget,
Yet I will not forget you.
See, I have inscribed you on the palms of My hands;
Your walls are continually before Me."

ISAIAH 49:15–16

The Lord will not cast off His people,
Nor will He forsake His inheritance.

PSALM 94:14

In You, O Lord, I put my trust;
Let me never be ashamed;
Deliver me in Your righteousness.
Bow down Your ear to me,
Deliver me speedily;
Be my rock of refuge,
A fortress of defense to save me.

For You are my rock and my fortress;
Therefore, for Your name's sake,
Lead me and guide me.
Pull me out of the net which they have secretly laid
        for me,
For You are my strength.
Into Your hand I commit my spirit;
You have redeemed me, O Lord God of truth.

PSALM 31:1–5

GOD PROMISES TO HEAL YOUR UNFORGIVENESS

As the elect of God, holy and beloved, put on tender mercies, kindness, humility, meekness, longsuffering; bearing with one another, and forgiving one another, if anyone has a complaint against another; even as Christ forgave you, so you also must do. But above all these things put on love, which is the bond of perfection.

COLOSSIANS 3:12–14

"If you forgive men their trespasses, your heavenly Father will also forgive you. But if you do not forgive men their trespasses, neither will your Father forgive your trespasses."

MATTHEW 6:14–15

We know Him who said, "Vengeance is Mine, I will repay," says the Lord. And again, "The LORD will judge His people."

HEBREWS 10:30

Peter came to [Jesus] and said, "Lord, how often shall my brother sin against me, and I forgive him? Up to seven times?"

Jesus said to him, "I do not say to you, up to seven times, but up to seventy times seven."

MATTHEW 18:21–22

"If your brother sins against you, rebuke him; and if he repents, forgive him. And if he sins against you seven times in a day, and seven times in a day returns to you, saying, 'I repent,' you shall forgive him."

LUKE 17:3-4

"Whenever you stand praying, if you have anything against anyone, forgive him, that your Father in heaven may also forgive you your trespasses. But if you do not forgive, neither will your Father in heaven forgive your trespasses."

MARK 11:25-26

"Blessed are those who are persecuted for righteousness'
sake,
For theirs is the kingdom of heaven.

"Blessed are you when they revile and persecute you, and say all kinds of evil against you falsely for My sake. Rejoice and be exceedingly glad, for great is your reward in heaven, for so they persecuted the prophets who were before you."

MATTHEW 5:10-12

GOD PROMISES TO HEAL YOU
WHEN YOU FEEL BETRAYED

Love suffers long and is kind; love does not envy; love does not parade itself, is not puffed up; does not behave rudely, does not seek its own, is not provoked, thinks no evil; does not rejoice in iniquity, but rejoices in the truth; bears all things, believes all things, hopes all things, endures all things.

1 CORINTHIANS 13:4–7

You, O LORD, are a shield for me,
My glory and the One who lifts up my head.
I cried to the LORD with my voice,
And He heard me from His holy hill. *Selah*

I lay down and slept;
I awoke, for the LORD sustained me.
I will not be afraid of ten thousands of people
Who have set themselves against me all around.

PSALM 3:3–6

Then David said to his son Solomon, "Be strong. Have strength of heart, and do it. Do not be afraid or troubled, for the Lord God, my God, is with you. He will not stop helping you. He will not leave you until all the work of the house of the Lord is finished."

1 CHRONICLES 28:20 NLV

Be of the same mind toward one another. Do not set your mind on high things, but associate with the humble. Do not be wise in your own opinion.

Repay no one evil for evil. Have regard for good things in the sight of all men. If it is possible, as much as depends on you, live peaceably with all men. Beloved, do not avenge yourselves, but rather give place to wrath; for it is written, "Vengeance is Mine, I will repay," says the Lord.

ROMANS 12:16–19

"Be merciful, just as your Father also is merciful.

"Judge not, and you shall not be judged. Condemn not, and you shall not be condemned. Forgive, and you will be forgiven."

LUKE 6:36–37

GOD PROMISES TO HEAL YOU WHEN

YOU ARE FACING A CRISIS

I love you, LORD, my strength.
The LORD is my rock, my fortress and my deliverer;
my God is my rock, in whom I take refuge,
my shield and the horn of my salvation, my stronghold.
I called to the LORD, who is worthy of praise,
and I have been saved from my enemies. . . .
In my distress I called to the LORD;
I cried to my God for help.
From his temple he heard my voice;
my cry came before him, into his ears. . . .
They confronted me in the day of my disaster,
but the LORD was my support.
He brought me out into a spacious place;
he rescued me because he delighted in me.

PSALM 18:1–3, 6, 18–19 NIV

I will call upon God,
And the LORD shall save me.
Evening and morning and at noon
I will pray, and cry aloud,
And He shall hear my voice.

PSALM 55:16–17

Give ear, O LORD, to my prayer;
And attend to the voice of my supplications.
In the day of my trouble I will call upon You,
For You will answer me.

Among the gods there is none like You, O Lord;
Nor are there any works like Your works.
All nations whom You have made
Shall come and worship before You, O Lord,
And shall glorify Your name.
For You are great, and do wondrous things;
You alone are God.

PSALM 86:6–10

[Cast] all your care upon Him, for He cares for you.

Be sober, be vigilant; because your adversary the devil walks about like a roaring lion, seeking whom he may devour. Resist him, steadfast in the faith, knowing that the same sufferings are experienced by your brotherhood in the world. But may the God of all grace, who called us to His eternal glory by Christ Jesus, after you have suffered a while, perfect, establish, strengthen, and settle you.

1 PETER 5:7–10

The LORD is your keeper;
The LORD is your shade at your right hand.
The sun shall not strike you by day,
Nor the moon by night.

The LORD shall preserve you from all evil;
He shall preserve your soul.
The LORD shall preserve your going out and your coming
    in
From this time forth, and even forevermore.

PSALM 121:5–8

GOD'S PROMISES IN ACTION

Which Bible promises from this section do you want to
commit to memory?

....

....

....

....

Which relationships are you struggling with right now that
need God's attention?

....

....

....

....

Which people in your life can help you deepen your relationship with God?

....

....

....

....

GOD PROMISES HELP WITH YOUR FINANCIAL SITUATION

CHRISTINE CAINE ON HANDLING CRISIS

Fear can diminish our willingness to risk. To dream. To try again. To believe again. Instead of declaring, we question. Instead of standing, we shrink. Instead of persevering, we quit. Instead of trusting, we worry. . . .

If you've ever endured one crisis after another—if you've ever felt hammered by the enemy—then you know what I'm talking about. If you've ever watched a loved one suffer a long-term illness or addiction, you've seen the "one step forward, two steps backward" rhythm that can happen. You know the challenge of believing for the best, while probably being told to prepare for the worst. You know what it's like to courageously cling to your faith, while gradually being conditioned by unexpected events to live in fear. . . .

But fear is not from God, and it's not more powerful than God. He knew it would come to steal our peace, not once or twice, but constantly throughout our lives. So, in his great mercy and faithfulness to us, God made a way for us to be more than equipped to overcome its effects and walk in faith. He gave us three offensive weapons to lean into when we're attacked: "For God has not given us a spirit of fear, but of *power* and of *love* and of *a sound mind*" (2 Timothy 1:7 NKJV, emphasis added). . . .

Why love? Because [God] is love, and he is the greatest power of all.

—Unexpected[6]

Remember the LORD *your God.*

He is the one who gives you

power to be successful, in order to

fulfill the covenant he confirmed

to your ancestors with an oath.

DEUTERONOMY 8:18 NLT

GOD PROMISES HELP WHEN YOU'RE UNEMPLOYED

Oh, taste and see that the LORD is good;
Blessed is the man who trusts in Him!
Oh, fear the LORD, you His saints!
There is no want to those who fear Him.
The young lions lack and suffer hunger;
But those who seek the LORD shall not lack any good
    thing.

PSALM 34:8–10

My son, give attention to my words;
Incline your ear to my sayings.
Do not let them depart from your eyes;
Keep them in the midst of your heart;
For they are life to those who find them,
And health to all their flesh.
Keep your heart with all diligence,
For out of it spring the issues of life.

PROVERBS 4:20–23

O LORD, You have searched me and known me.
You know my sitting down and my rising up;
You understand my thought afar off.
You comprehend my path and my lying down,

And are acquainted with all my ways.
For there is not a word on my tongue,
But behold, O Lord, You know it altogether.
You have hedged me behind and before,
And laid Your hand upon me.
Such knowledge is too wonderful for me;
It is high, I cannot attain it.

Where can I go from Your Spirit?
Or where can I flee from Your presence?
If I ascend into heaven, You are there;
If I make my bed in hell, behold, You are there.
If I take the wings of the morning,
And dwell in the uttermost parts of the sea,
Even there Your hand shall lead me,
And Your right hand shall hold me.
If I say, "Surely the darkness shall fall on me,"
Even the night shall be light about me;
Indeed, the darkness shall not hide from You,
But the night shines as the day;
The darkness and the light are both alike to You. . . .

Search me, O God, and know my heart;
Try me, and know my anxieties;
And see if there is any wicked way in me,
And lead me in the way everlasting.

PSALM 139:1–12, 23–24

I know the thoughts that I think toward you, says the LORD, thoughts of peace and not of evil, to give you a future and a hope. Then you will call upon Me and go and pray to Me, and I will listen to you. And you will seek Me and find Me, when you search for Me with all your heart.

JEREMIAH 29:11–13

"If there is among you a poor man of your brethren, within any of the gates in your land which the LORD your God is giving you, you shall not harden your heart nor shut your hand from your poor brother, but you shall open your hand wide to him and willingly lend him sufficient for his need, whatever he needs."

DEUTERONOMY 15:7–8

The LORD is my shepherd;
I shall not want.
He makes me to lie down in green pastures;
He leads me beside the still waters.
He restores my soul;
He leads me in the paths of righteousness
For His name's sake.

PSALM 23:1–3

GOD PROMISES HELP WHEN YOU
HAVE FINANCIAL HARDSHIP

"Do not worry, saying, 'What shall we eat?' or 'What shall we drink?' or 'What shall we wear?' For after all these things the Gentiles seek. For your heavenly Father knows that you need all these things. But seek first the kingdom of God and His righteousness, and all these things shall be added to you."

MATTHEW 6:31–33

Now to Him who is able to do exceedingly abundantly above all that we ask or think, according to the power that works in us.

EPHESIANS 3:20

Blessed is the one who perseveres under trial because, having stood the test, that person will receive the crown of life that the Lord has promised to those who love him.

JAMES 1:12 NIV

"Give, and it will be given to you: good measure, pressed down, shaken together, and running over will be put into your bosom. For with the same measure that you use, it will be measured back to you."

LUKE 6:38

This I say: He who sows sparingly will also reap sparingly, and he who sows bountifully will also reap bountifully. So let each one give as he purposes in his heart, not grudgingly or of necessity; for God loves a cheerful giver. And God is able to make all grace abound toward you, that you, always having all sufficiency in all things, may have an abundance for every good work.

2 CORINTHIANS 9:6–8

My God shall supply all your need according to His riches in glory by Christ Jesus.

PHILIPPIANS 4:19

I have been young, and now am old;
Yet I have not seen the righteous forsaken,
Nor his descendants begging bread.
He is ever merciful, and lends;
And his descendants are blessed.

PSALM 37:25–26

The blessing of the LORD makes one rich,
And He adds no sorrow with it.

PROVERBS 10:22

GOD PROMISES HELP WHEN YOU LACK CONFIDENCE

[The Lord] said to me, "My grace is sufficient for you, for my power is made perfect in weakness." Therefore I will boast all the more gladly of my weaknesses, so that the power of Christ may rest upon me.

2 CORINTHIANS 12:9 ESV

Though an army may encamp against me,
My heart shall not fear;
Though war may rise against me,
In this I will be confident.

PSALM 27:3

The LORD God is my strength;
He will make my feet like deer's feet,
And He will make me walk on my high hills.

HABAKKUK 3:19

Do not be afraid of sudden terror,
Nor of trouble from the wicked when it comes;
For the LORD will be your confidence,
And will keep your foot from being caught.

PROVERBS 3:25–26

Now this is the confidence that we have in Him, that if we ask anything according to His will, He hears us. And if we know that He hears us, whatever we ask, we know that we have the petitions that we have asked of Him.

1 JOHN 5:14–15

The LORD will guide you continually,
And satisfy your soul in drought,
And strengthen your bones;
You shall be like a watered garden,
And like a spring of water, whose waters do not fail.

ISAIAH 58:11

If God is for us, who can be against us? He who did not spare His own Son, but delivered Him up for us all, how shall He not with Him also freely give us all things? Who shall bring a charge against God's elect? It is God who justifies. Who is he who condemns? It is Christ who died, and furthermore is also risen, who is even at the right hand of God, who also makes intercession for us. Who shall separate us from the love of Christ? Shall tribulation, or distress, or persecution, or famine, or nakedness, or peril, or sword? . . . In all these things we are more than conquerors through Him who loved us.

ROMANS 8:31–35, 37

"Be strong and courageous; do not be afraid nor dismayed before the king of Assyria, nor before all the multitude that is with him; for there are more with us than with him. With him is an arm of flesh; but with us is the Lord our God, to help us and to fight our battles." And the people were strengthened by the words of Hezekiah king of Judah.

2 CHRONICLES 32:7–8

Through Christ you have come to trust in God. And you have placed your faith and hope in God because he raised Christ from the dead and gave him great glory.

You were cleansed from your sins when you obeyed the truth, so now you must show sincere love to each other as brothers and sisters. Love each other deeply with all your heart.

For you have been born again, but not to a life that will quickly end. Your new life will last forever because it comes from the eternal, living word of God. As the Scriptures say,

"People are like grass;
their beauty is like a flower in the field.
The grass withers and the flower fades.
But the word of the Lord remains forever."

And that word is the Good News that was preached to you.

1 PETER 1:21–25 NLT

GOD PROMISES HELP WHEN YOUR
WORLD IS TURNED UPSIDE DOWN

Jesus answered them, "Do you now believe? Indeed the hour is coming, yes, has now come, that you will be scattered, each to his own, and will leave Me alone. And yet I am not alone, because the Father is with Me.

"These things I have spoken to you, that in Me you may have peace. In the world you will have tribulation; but be of good cheer, I have overcome the world."

JOHN 16:31–33

My brethren, count it all joy when you fall into various trials, knowing that the testing of your faith produces patience. But let patience have its perfect work, that you may be perfect and complete, lacking nothing. If any of you lacks wisdom, let him ask of God, who gives to all liberally and without reproach, and it will be given to him.

JAMES 1:2–5

Blessed is the man
Who walks not in the counsel of the ungodly,
Nor stands in the path of sinners,
Nor sits in the seat of the scornful;
But his delight is in the law of the LORD,
And in His law he meditates day and night.
He shall be like a tree
Planted by the rivers of water,
That brings forth its fruit in its season,
Whose leaf also shall not wither;
And whatever he does shall prosper.

The ungodly are not so,
But are like the chaff which the wind drives away.
Therefore the ungodly shall not stand in the judgment,
Nor sinners in the congregation of the righteous.

For the LORD knows the way of the righteous,
But the way of the ungodly shall perish.

PSALM 1:1–6

Therefore we do not lose heart. Even though our outward man is perishing, yet the inward man is being renewed day by day. For our light affliction, which is but for a moment, is working for us a far more exceeding and eternal weight of glory, while we do not look at the things which are seen, but at the things which are not seen. For the things which are seen are temporary, but the things which are not seen are eternal.

2 CORINTHIANS 4:16–18

Let love be without hypocrisy. Abhor what is evil. Cling to what is good. Be kindly affectionate to one another with brotherly love, in honor giving preference to one another; not lagging in diligence, fervent in spirit, serving the Lord; rejoicing in hope, patient in tribulation, continuing steadfastly in prayer.

ROMANS 12:9–12

In everything give thanks; for this is the will of God in Christ Jesus for you.

Do not quench the Spirit. Do not despise prophecies. Test all things; hold fast what is good. Abstain from every form of evil.

1 THESSALONIANS 5:18–22

GOD PROMISES HELP TO KNOW
THAT JESUS IS ENOUGH

By his divine power, God has given us everything we need for living a godly life. We have received all of this by coming to know him, the one who called us to himself by means of his marvelous glory and excellence.

2 PETER 1:3 NLT

Jesus said to [the people], "I am the bread of life. He who comes to Me shall never hunger, and he who believes in Me shall never thirst."

JOHN 6:35

Let your conduct be without covetousness; be content with such things as you have. For He Himself has said, "I will never leave you nor forsake you." So we may boldly say:
> "The LORD is my helper;
> I will not fear.
> What can man do to me?" . . .

Jesus Christ is the same yesterday, today, and forever.

HEBREWS 13:5–6, 8

For the love of money is a root of all kinds of evil, for which some have strayed from the faith in their greediness, and pierced themselves through with many sorrows. But you, O man of God, flee these things and pursue righteousness, godliness, faith, love, patience, gentleness.

1 TIMOTHY 6:10–11

In [Jesus] dwells all the fullness of the Godhead bodily; and you are complete in Him, who is the head of all principality and power.

COLOSSIANS 2:9–10

[The resurrected] Jesus came and spoke to [the eleven disciples], saying, "All authority has been given to Me in heaven and on earth. Go therefore and make disciples of all the nations, baptizing them in the name of the Father and of the Son and of the Holy Spirit, teaching them to observe all things that I have commanded you; and lo, I am with you always, even to the end of the age." Amen.

MATTHEW 28:18–20

"This is the 'stone which was rejected by you builders, which has become the chief cornerstone.' Nor is there salvation in any other, for there is no other name under heaven given among men by which we must be saved."

ACTS 4:11–12

GOD'S PROMISES IN ACTION

Which Bible promises from this section do you want to commit to memory?

....

....

....

....

Which financial issues in your life do you need to trust God to handle?

....

....

....

....

Which financial situations prevent you from deepening your relationship with God? What can you do to change that?

....

....

....

....

GOD PROMISES TO BE
THERE IN YOUR SORROW

LYSA TERKEURST ON PERSEVERANCE

God loves us too much to answer our prayers in any other way than the right way. And He loves us too much to answer our prayers at any other time than the right time.

The process will most likely require us to be persevering. Patient. Maybe even longsuffering.

Longsuffering. It's not a word I want to be part of my story. But as my friends have prayed for me, this word keeps bubbling up. Longsuffering means having or showing patience despite troubles, especially those caused by other people. . . .

When we think the process of longsuffering is unbearable, we must remember it would be deadly for God to put us up on that solid rock before we are strong, firm, and steadfast. And it would be cruel for Him to require us to sing before we have a song.

There is purpose to this process. Yes, the process will be so messy, so full of slime and mud and mire and cries for help that you can't help but wonder whether they are being heard or not.

They are. . . . God isn't far off. He's just far more interested in your being prepared than in your being comfortable. God will take every cry you've uttered and arrange those sounds into a glorious song. He will add it to His symphony of compassion.

—*It's Not Supposed to Be This Way*[7]

I waited patiently for the Lord;

he turned to me and heard my cry.

He lifted me out of the slimy pit,

out of the mud and mire;

he set my feet on a rock

and gave me a firm place to stand.

He put a new song in my mouth,

a hymn of praise to our God.

Many will see and fear the Lord

and put their trust in him.

PSALM 40:1–3 NIV

GOD PROMISES TO BE THERE WHEN
GRIEF OVERWHELMS YOU

Blessed be the God and Father of our Lord Jesus Christ, the Father of mercies and God of all comfort, who comforts us in all our tribulation, that we may be able to comfort those who are in any trouble, with the comfort with which we ourselves are comforted by God.

2 CORINTHIANS 1:3–4

[Since] we believe that Jesus died and rose again, even so God will bring with Him those who sleep in Jesus.

1 THESSALONIANS 4:14

Now may our Lord Jesus Christ Himself, and our God and Father, who has loved us and given us everlasting consolation and good hope by grace, comfort your hearts and establish you in every good word and work.

2 THESSALONIANS 2:16–17

"Blessed are those who mourn,
For they shall be comforted."

MATTHEW 5:4

"O Death, where is your sting?
O Hades, where is your victory?"

1 CORINTHIANS 15:55

I heard a loud voice from heaven saying, "Behold, the tabernacle of God is with men, and He will dwell with them, and they shall be His people. God Himself will be with them and be their God. And God will wipe away every tear from their eyes; there shall be no more death, nor sorrow, nor crying. There shall be no more pain, for the former things have passed away."

REVELATION 21:3–4

Remember the word to Your servant,
Upon which You have caused me to hope.
This is my comfort in my affliction,
For Your word has given me life.

PSALM 119:49–50

Jesus said to [Martha], "I am the resurrection and the life. He who believes in Me, though he may die, he shall live. And whoever lives and believes in Me shall never die. Do you believe this?"

JOHN 11:25–26

GOD PROMISES TO BE THERE WHEN YOU NEED TO SURRENDER

Without faith it is impossible to please Him, for he who comes to God must believe that He is, and that He is a rewarder of those who diligently seek Him.

HEBREWS 11:6

Present your bodies a living sacrifice, holy, acceptable to God, which is your reasonable service. And do not be conformed to this world, but be transformed by the renewing of your mind, that you may prove what is that good and acceptable and perfect will of God.

ROMANS 12:1–2

If you forsake the LORD and serve foreign gods, then He will turn and do you harm and consume you, after He has done you good.

JOSHUA 24:20

Let us continually offer the sacrifice of praise to God, that is, the fruit of our lips, giving thanks to His name. But do not forget to do good and to share, for with such sacrifices God is well pleased.

HEBREWS 13:15–16

"Everyone who is called by My name,
Whom I have created for My glory;
I have formed him, yes, I have made him. . . .

"This people I have formed for Myself;
They shall declare My praise."

ISAIAH 43:7, 21

"The hour is coming, and now is, when the true worshipers will worship the Father in spirit and truth; for the Father is seeking such to worship Him. God is Spirit, and those who worship Him must worship in spirit and truth."

JOHN 4:23–24

You also, as living stones, are being built up a spiritual house, a holy priesthood, to offer up spiritual sacrifices acceptable to God through Jesus Christ. . . .

You are a chosen generation, a royal priesthood, a holy nation, His own special people, that you may proclaim the praises of Him who called you out of darkness into His marvelous light.

1 PETER 2:5, 9

I exhort first of all that supplications, prayers, intercessions, and giving of thanks be made for all men . . . for this is good and acceptable in the sight of God our Savior. . . .

I desire therefore that the men pray everywhere, lifting up holy hands, without wrath and doubting.

1 TIMOTHY 2:1, 3, 8

I have been crucified with Christ; it is no longer I who live, but Christ lives in me; and the life which I now live in the flesh I live by faith in the Son of God, who loved me and gave Himself for me.

GALATIANS 2:20

Therefore humble yourselves under the mighty hand of God, that He may exalt you in due time.

1 PETER 5:6

Humble yourselves in the sight of the Lord, and He will lift you up.

JAMES 4:10

GOD PROMISES TO BE THERE WHEN
YOU WANT TO GIVE UP

Seeing then that we have a great High Priest who has passed through the heavens, Jesus the Son of God, let us hold fast our confession. For we do not have a High Priest who cannot sympathize with our weaknesses, but was in all points tempted as we are, yet without sin. Let us therefore come boldly to the throne of grace, that we may obtain mercy and find grace to help in time of need.

HEBREWS 4:14–16

I have learned in whatever state I am, to be content: I know how to be abased, and I know how to abound. Everywhere and in all things I have learned both to be full and to be hungry, both to abound and to suffer need. I can do all things through Christ who strengthens me.

PHILIPPIANS 4:11–13

Consider Him who endured such hostility from sinners against Himself, lest you become weary and discouraged in your souls.

HEBREWS 12:3

Thanks be to God, who gives us the victory through our Lord Jesus Christ.

Therefore, my beloved brethren, be steadfast, immovable, always abounding in the work of the Lord, knowing that your labor is not in vain in the Lord.

1 CORINTHIANS 15:57–58

"Fear not, for I am with you;
Be not dismayed, for I am your God.
I will strengthen you,
Yes, I will help you,
I will uphold you with My righteous right hand."

ISAIAH 41:10

"Behold, I have created the blacksmith
Who blows the coals in the fire,
Who brings forth an instrument for his work;
And I have created the spoiler to destroy.
No weapon formed against you shall prosper,
And every tongue which rises against you in judgment
You shall condemn.
This is the heritage of the servants of the LORD,
And their righteousness is from Me,"
Says the LORD.

ISAIAH 54:16–17

GOD PROMISES TO BE THERE WHEN
YOU DISCOVER FORGIVENESS

There is . . . now no condemnation to those who are in Christ Jesus, who do not walk according to the flesh, but according to the Spirit. For the law of the Spirit of life in Christ Jesus has made me free from the law of sin and death.

ROMANS 8:1–2

You, brethren, have been called to liberty; only do not use liberty as an opportunity for the flesh, but through love serve one another.

GALATIANS 5:13

"Whoever desires to save his life will lose it, but whoever loses his life for My sake will find it. For what profit is it to a man if he gains the whole world, and loses his own soul? Or what will a man give in exchange for his soul?"

MATTHEW 16:25–26

Stand fast therefore in the liberty by which Christ has made us free, and do not be entangled again with a yoke of bondage.

GALATIANS 5:1

Jesus said to those Jews who believed Him, "If you abide in My word, you are My disciples indeed. And you shall know the truth, and the truth shall make you free. . . .

"If the Son makes you free, you shall be free indeed."

JOHN 8:31–32, 36

He who looks into the perfect law of liberty and continues in it, and is not a forgetful hearer but a doer of the work, this one will be blessed in what he does.

JAMES 1:25

Let the sinful turn from his way, and the one who does not know God turn from his thoughts. Let him turn to the Lord, and He will have loving-pity on him. Let him turn to our God, for He will for sure forgive all his sins.

ISAIAH 55:7 NLV

But you must be sorry for your sins and turn from them. You must turn to God and have your sins taken away. Then many times your soul will receive new strength from the Lord. He will send Jesus back to the world. He is the Christ Who long ago was chosen for you.

ACTS 3:19–20 NLV

GOD PROMISES TO BE THERE
WHEN YOU NEED PEACE

I am being held in prison because of working for the Lord. I ask you from my heart to live and work the way the Lord expected you to live and work. Live and work without pride. Be gentle and kind. Do not be hard on others. Let love keep you from doing that. Work hard to live together as one by the help of the Holy Spirit. Then there will be peace.

EPHESIANS 4:1–3 NLV

You will keep him in perfect peace,
Whose mind is stayed on You,
Because he trusts in You.

ISAIAH 26:3

Now may the Lord of peace Himself give you peace always in every way. The Lord be with you all.

2 THESSALONIANS 3:16

I will both lie down in peace, and sleep;
For You alone, O LORD, make me dwell in safety.

PSALM 4:8

"Peace I leave with you, My peace I give to you; not as the world gives do I give to you. Let not your heart be troubled, neither let it be afraid."

JOHN 14:27

But the fruit of the Spirit is love, joy, peace, longsuffering, kindness, goodness, faithfulness, gentleness, self-control. Against such there is no law.

GALATIANS 5:22–23

The work of righteousness will be peace,
And the effect of righteousness, quietness and assurance
   forever.

ISAIAH 32:17

For unto us a Child is born,
Unto us a Son is given;
And the government will be upon His shoulder.
And His name will be called
Wonderful, Counselor, Mighty God,
Everlasting Father, Prince of Peace.

ISAIAH 9:6

GOD'S PROMISES IN ACTION

Which Bible promises from this section do you want to
commit to memory?

....

....

....

....

What sorrow or grief are you struggling with right now that
God wants to help you with?

....

....

....

....

As you're grieving or feeling sadness, what can you do to
deepen your relationship with God?

....

....

....

....

GOD PROMISES TO LOOK AFTER YOUR HEALTH AND WELL-BEING

BILLY GRAHAM ON SUFFERING

Sometimes we have hurts that are too deep and sensitive for others to see or help.

But who except God Himself can scan the invisible me—my heart, my soul, my spirit? There are hurts in our personalities too deep and too complicated for even the most sophisticated modern techniques to diagnose or to solve.

Only God Himself who made us understands us fully. . . . Only God can diagnose our problem accurately and will show us how to solve it; and when there is no solution, He will give us the grace to live with it. . . .

God wants to help us when we suffer. He can give His *presence* for comfort, His *power* for endurance, His *purpose* so that we might gain insight into our situation. And He can produce within us valuable qualities that will strengthen and mold our lives.

God can help us because He alone knows *why* we are suffering and *where* the suffering can take us.

He can also help us because *He* knows *what* it means to suffer. When we go through difficult times and turn to someone for counsel and comfort, we seek someone who can understand—someone who has experienced a similar situation and can relate to our feelings.

God can relate to us because He has suffered in the person of His Son.

—*Who's in Charge of a World That Suffers?*[8]

For I consider that the sufferings of this present time are not worthy to be compared with the glory which shall be revealed in us.

ROMANS 8:18

GOD PROMISES TO HEAL YOU

To you who fear My name
The Sun of Righteousness shall arise
With healing in His wings."

MALACHI 4:2

O LORD my God, I cried out to You,
And You healed me.
O LORD, You brought my soul up from the grave;
You have kept me alive.

PSALM 30:2–3

[The LORD] heals the brokenhearted
And binds up their wounds.
He counts the number of the stars;
He calls them all by name.
Great is our Lord, and mighty in power;
His understanding is infinite.
The LORD lifts up the humble;
He casts the wicked down to the ground.

PSALM 147:3–6

"The Spirit of the Lord GOD is upon Me,
Because the LORD has anointed Me . . .
To comfort all who mourn,
To console those who mourn in Zion,
To give them beauty for ashes,
The oil of joy for mourning,
The garment of praise for the spirit of heaviness;
That they may be called trees of righteousness,
The planting of the LORD, that He may be glorified."

ISAIAH 61:1–3

Then great multitudes came to [Jesus], having with them the lame, blind, mute, maimed, and many others; and they laid them down at Jesus' feet, and He healed them.

MATTHEW 15:30

Is anyone among you sick? Let him call for the elders of the church, and let them pray over him, anointing him with oil in the name of the Lord. And the prayer of faith will save the sick, and the Lord will raise him up. And if he has committed sins, he will be forgiven. Confess your trespasses to one another, and pray for one another, that you may be healed. The effective, fervent prayer of a righteous man avails much.

JAMES 5:14–16

"The Spirit of the LORD is upon Me,
Because He has anointed Me
To preach the gospel to the poor;
He has sent Me to heal the brokenhearted,
To proclaim liberty to the captives
And recovery of sight to the blind,
To set at liberty those who are oppressed;
To proclaim the acceptable year of the LORD."

LUKE 4:18-19

"So you shall serve the LORD your God, and He will bless your bread and your water. And I will take sickness away from the midst of you."

EXODUS 23:25

"For I will restore health to you
And heal you of your wounds," says the LORD.

JEREMIAH 30:17

And when Jesus went out He saw a great multitude; and He was moved with compassion for them, and healed their sick.

MATTHEW 14:14

GOD PROMISES TO HEAL YOUR EXHAUSTION

And let us not grow weary while doing good, for in due season we shall reap if we do not lose heart.

GALATIANS 6:9

Wait on the LORD,
And keep His way,
And He shall exalt you to inherit the land;
When the wicked are cut off, you shall see it.
I have seen the wicked in great power,
And spreading himself like a native green tree.
Yet he passed away, and behold, he was no more;
Indeed I sought him, but he could not be found.

The salvation of the righteous is from the LORD;
He is their strength in the time of trouble.
And the LORD shall help them and deliver them;
He shall deliver them from the wicked,
And save them,
Because they trust in Him.

PSALM 37:34–36, 39–40

"Take My yoke upon you and learn from Me, for I am gentle and lowly in heart, and you will find rest for your souls. For My yoke is easy and My burden is light."

MATTHEW 11:29–30

"For I give plenty of water to the weary ones, and refresh everyone who languishes."

JEREMIAH 31:25 NASB

For thus says the High and Lofty One
Who inhabits eternity, whose name is Holy:
"I dwell in the high and holy place,
With him who has a contrite and humble spirit,
To revive the spirit of the humble,
And to revive the heart of the contrite ones. . . .
I have seen his ways, and will heal him;
I will also lead him,
And restore comforts to him
And to his mourners.

"I create the fruit of the lips:
Peace, peace to him who is far off and to him who
        is near,"
Says the LORD,
"And I will heal him."

ISAIAH 57:15, 18–19

Now He was telling them a parable to show that at all times they ought to pray and not become discouraged.

LUKE 18:1 NASB

Then Moses said to the LORD . . . "Now therefore, I pray, if I have found grace in Your sight, show me now Your way, that I may know You and that I may find grace in Your sight. And consider that this nation is Your people."

And He said, "My Presence will go with you, and I will give you rest."

EXODUS 33:12–14

"'It is a sign between Me and the children of Israel forever; for in six days the LORD made the heavens and the earth, and on the seventh day He rested and was refreshed.'"

EXODUS 31:17

"Come to Me, all you who labor and are heavy laden, and I will give you rest."

MATTHEW 11:28

GOD PROMISES TO HEAL YOUR STRESS

Bless the LORD, O my soul;
And all that is within me, bless His holy name!
Bless the LORD, O my soul,
And forget not all His benefits:
Who forgives all your iniquities,
Who heals all your diseases,
Who redeems your life from destruction,
Who crowns you with lovingkindness and tender
    mercies,
Who satisfies your mouth with good things,
So that your youth is renewed like the eagle's.

                              PSALM 103:1–5

The LORD builds up Jerusalem;
He gathers together the outcasts of Israel.
He heals the brokenhearted
And binds up their wounds.
He counts the number of the stars;
He calls them all by name.
Great is our Lord, and mighty in power;
His understanding is infinite.

                              PSALM 147:2–5

Anxiety weighs down the heart, but a kind word cheers
it up.

PROVERBS 12:25 NIV

I have set the LORD always before me;
Because He is at my right hand I shall not be moved.

PSALM 16:8

I will bless the LORD at all times;
His praise shall continually be in my mouth.
My soul shall make its boast in the LORD;
The humble shall hear of it and be glad.
Oh, magnify the LORD with me,
And let us exalt His name together.

I sought the LORD, and He heard me,
And delivered me from all my fears.

PSALM 34:1–4

Can any one of you by worrying add a single hour to
your life?

MATTHEW 6:27 NIV

GOD PROMISES TO HEAL YOUR PHYSICAL ILLNESS

Beloved, I pray that you may prosper in all things and be in health, just as your soul prospers.

3 JOHN 1:2

Then Jesus went about all the cities and villages, teaching in their synagogues, preaching the gospel of the kingdom, and healing every sickness and every disease among the people.

MATTHEW 9:35

And the whole multitude sought to touch Him, for power went out from Him and healed them all.

LUKE 6:19

Who Himself bore our sins in His own body on the tree, that we, having died to sins, might live for righteousness—by whose stripes you were healed.

1 PETER 2:24

Heal me, O Lord, and I shall be healed;
Save me, and I shall be saved,
For You are my praise.

JEREMIAH 17:14

But He was wounded for our transgressions,
He was bruised for our iniquities;
The chastisement for our peace was upon Him,
And by His stripes we are healed.

ISAIAH 53:5

"If you diligently heed the voice of the LORD your God and do what is right in His sight, give ear to His commandments and keep all His statutes, I will put none of the diseases on you which I have brought on the Egyptians. For I am the LORD who heals you."

EXODUS 15:26

"And these signs will follow those who believe: In My name they will cast out demons; they will speak with new tongues; they will take up serpents; and if they drink anything deadly, it will by no means hurt them; they will lay hands on the sick, and they will recover."

MARK 16:17–18

And when He had called His twelve disciples to Him, He gave them power over unclean spirits, to cast them out, and to heal all kinds of sickness and all kinds of disease.

MATTHEW 10:1

GOD PROMISES TO HEAL YOU SPIRITUALLY

Blessed is he who considers the poor;
The Lord will deliver him in time of trouble.
The Lord will preserve him and keep him alive,
And he will be blessed on the earth;
You will not deliver him to the will of his enemies.
The Lord will strengthen him on his bed of illness;
You will sustain him on his sickbed.

PSALM 41:1–3

One thing I do, forgetting those things which are behind and reaching forward to those things which are ahead, I press toward the goal for the prize of the upward call of God in Christ Jesus.

PHILIPPIANS 3:13–14

He who covers his sins will not prosper,
But whoever confesses and forsakes them will have
mercy.

PROVERBS 28:13

Have you not known?

Have you not heard?

The everlasting God, the LORD,

The Creator of the ends of the earth,

Neither faints nor is weary.

His understanding is unsearchable.

He gives power to the weak,

And to those who have no might He increases strength.

ISAIAH 40:28–29

"I will seek what was lost and bring back what was driven away, bind up the broken and strengthen what was sick; but I will destroy the fat and the strong, and feed them in judgment. . . .

"Thus they shall know that I, the LORD their God, am with them, and they, the house of Israel, are My people," says the Lord GOD.

"You are My flock, the flock of My pasture; you are men, and I am your God," says the Lord GOD.

EZEKIEL 34:16, 30–31

No temptation has overtaken you except such as is common to man; but God is faithful, who will not allow you to be tempted beyond what you are able, but with the temptation will also make the way of escape, that you may be able to bear it.

1 CORINTHIANS 10:13

Have mercy on me, O LORD, for I am weak;
O LORD, heal me, for my bones are troubled.
My soul also is greatly troubled;
But You, O LORD—how long?

Return, O LORD, deliver me!
Oh, save me for Your mercies' sake! . . .

I am weary with my groaning;
All night I make my bed swim;
I drench my couch with my tears.
My eye wastes away because of grief;
It grows old because of all my enemies.

Depart from me, all you workers of iniquity;
For the LORD has heard the voice of my weeping.
The LORD has heard my supplication;
The LORD will receive my prayer.

PSALM 6:2-4, 6-9

Also a multitude gathered from the surrounding cities to
Jerusalem, bringing sick people and those who were tormented by
unclean spirits, and they were all healed.

ACTS 5:16

GOD'S PROMISES IN ACTION

Which Bible promises from this section do you want to commit to memory?

....

....

....

....

What health issues might you be struggling with (physical, mental, spiritual) that you need to take to God in prayer?

....

....

....

....

Healing requires trusting God's unfailing love. How can you deepen your relationship with God as your healing continues?

....

....

....

....

GOD PROMISES TO CALM
YOUR UNCERTAINTY

ANN VOSKAMP ON FACING YOUR FEARS

Life is waves. Grief comes in waves. Suffering comes in waves. Losses come in waves. There is no controlling life's storms; there is only learning to live with waves. The real work of being human is mastering how to process losses while being in the process of moving forward. The real work of being human is trusting the way is the waves, right through the valleys and crests. . . .

Only what you actually name can you regulate. Only when you open up, name, express your fears, can the fears begin to ebb, which is why the Word asks us to calm our fears by putting words to them, by bringing them to the Word: "Do not be anxious about anything, but in every situation, by prayer and petition, with thanksgiving, present your requests to God. And the peace of God, which transcends all understanding, will guard your hearts and your minds in Christ Jesus" (Philippians 4:6–7 NIV). "Cast all your anxiety on him because he cares for you" (1 Peter 5:7 NIV). Jesus asks us to examine why we are so afraid because He knows: Fears can turn and burn our hearts so they ignite fight-or-flight responses, making our fears masquerade like anger, like control, like perfectionism, like procrastination, like self-harm, like a thousand other masked faces.

God knows no question may matter more than asking ourselves why we are so afraid . . . because God knows . . . fear is about losing what we love.

—*WayMaker*[9]

Whenever I am afraid,

I will trust in You.

In God (I will praise His word),

In God I have put my trust;

I will not fear.

What can flesh do to me?

PSALM 56:3-4

GOD PROMISES TO CALM YOUR FEARS

Surely God is my salvation;
    I will trust and not be afraid.
The LORD, the LORD himself, is my strength and my
       defense;
    he has become my salvation."
With joy you will draw water
    from the wells of salvation.

ISAIAH 12:2–3 NIV

For the vision is yet for an appointed time;
But at the end it will speak, and it will not lie.
Though it tarries, wait for it;
Because it will surely come,
It will not tarry.

HABAKKUK 2:3

Wait on the LORD;
Be of good courage,
And He shall strengthen your heart;
Wait, I say, on the LORD!

PSALM 27:14

"Who gave human beings their mouths? Who makes them deaf or mute? Who gives them sight or makes them blind? Is it not I, the LORD? Now go; I will help you speak and will teach you what to say."

EXODUS 4:11–12 NIV

For the Spirit God gave us does not make us timid, but gives us power, love and self-discipline.

2 TIMOTHY 1:7 NIV

Who is a God like you,
>   who pardons sin and forgives the transgression
>   of the remnant of his inheritance?
You do not stay angry forever
>   but delight to show mercy.
You will again have compassion on us;
>   you will tread our sins underfoot
>   and hurl all our iniquities into the depths of the sea.

MICAH 7:18–19 NIV

In God I have put my trust;
I will not be afraid.
What can man do to me?

PSALM 56:11

GOD PROMISES TO CALM YOUR RESTLESSNESS

When doubts filled my mind,
>   your comfort gave me renewed hope and cheer.
>
> PSALM 94:19 NLT

Those who live according to the flesh set their minds on the things of the flesh, but those who live according to the Spirit, the things of the Spirit. For to be carnally minded is death, but to be spiritually minded is life and peace.

> ROMANS 8:5–6

The kingdom of God is not eating and drinking, but righteousness and peace and joy in the Holy Spirit. For he who serves Christ in these things is acceptable to God and approved by men.

Therefore let us pursue the things which make for peace and the things by which one may edify another.

> ROMANS 14:17–19

Be of good comfort, be of one mind, live in peace; and the God of love and peace will be with you.

2 CORINTHIANS 13:11

The fear of the Lord leads to life,
And he who has it will abide in satisfaction;
He will not be visited with evil.

PROVERBS 19:23

Great peace have those who love Your law,
And nothing causes them to stumble.

PSALM 119:165

The righteous perishes,
And no man takes it to heart;
Merciful men are taken away,
While no one considers
That the righteous is taken away from evil.
He shall enter into peace;
They shall rest in their beds,
Each one walking in his uprightness.

ISAIAH 57:1–2

GOD PROMISES TO CALM YOUR WORRIES

There is no fear in love; but perfect love casts out fear, because fear involves torment. But he who fears has not been made perfect in love. We love Him because He first loved us.

1 JOHN 4:18–19

Even if you have to suffer for doing good things, God will bless you. So stop being afraid and don't worry about what people might do.

1 PETER 3:14 CEV

Put on love, which is the bond of perfection. And let the peace of God rule in your hearts, to which also you were called in one body; and be thankful.

COLOSSIANS 3:14–15

I receive joy when I am weak. I receive joy when people talk against me and make it hard for me and try to hurt me and make trouble for me. I receive joy when all these things come to me because of Christ. For when I am weak, then I am strong.

2 CORINTHIANS 12:10 NLV

Yea, though I walk through the valley of the shadow of
    death,
I will fear no evil;
For You are with me;
Your rod and Your staff, they comfort me.

You prepare a table before me in the presence of my
    enemies;
You anoint my head with oil;
My cup runs over.
Surely goodness and mercy shall follow me
All the days of my life;
And I will dwell in the house of the Lord
Forever.

PSALM 23:4–6

Say to those with fearful hearts,
    "Be strong, and do not fear,
for your God is coming to destroy your enemies.
    He is coming to save you."

ISAIAH 35:4 NLT

Then He said to His disciples, "Therefore I say to you, do not worry about your life, what you will eat; nor about the body, what you will put on. Life is more than food, and the body is more than clothing. Consider the ravens, for they neither sow nor reap, which have neither storehouse nor barn; and God feeds them. Of how much more value are you than the birds? And which of you by worrying can add one cubit to his stature? If you then are not able to do the least, why are you anxious for the rest? Consider the lilies, how they grow: they neither toil nor spin; and yet I say to you, even Solomon in all his glory was not arrayed like one of these. If then God so clothes the grass, which today is in the field and tomorrow is thrown into the oven, how much more will He clothe you, O you of little faith?"

LUKE 12:22–28

[Martha] had a sister called Mary, who also sat at Jesus' feet and heard His word. But Martha was distracted with much serving, and she approached Him and said, "Lord, do You not care that my sister has left me to serve alone? Therefore tell her to help me."

And Jesus answered and said to her, "Martha, Martha, you are worried and troubled about many things. But one thing is needed, and Mary has chosen that good part, which will not be taken away from her."

LUKE 10:39–42

GOD PROMISES TO CALM YOU WHEN
YOU'RE UNDER ATTACK

The Lord is my light and my salvation;
Whom shall I fear?
The Lord is the strength of my life;
Of whom shall I be afraid? . . .

For in the time of trouble
He shall hide me in His pavilion;
In the secret place of His tabernacle
He shall hide me;
He shall set me high upon a rock.

PSALM 27:1, 5

The fear of man brings a snare,
But whoever trusts in the Lord shall be safe.

PROVERBS 29:25

Put on all of God's armor so that you will be able to stand
firm against all strategies of the devil.

EPHESIANS 6:11 NLT

He who dwells in the secret place of the Most High
Shall abide under the shadow of the Almighty.
I will say of the LORD, "He is my refuge and my fortress;
My God, in Him I will trust."

Surely He shall deliver you from the snare of the fowler
And from the perilous pestilence.
He shall cover you with His feathers,
And under His wings you shall take refuge;
His truth shall be your shield and buckler.
You shall not be afraid of the terror by night,
Nor of the arrow that flies by day,
Nor of the pestilence that walks in darkness,
Nor of the destruction that lays waste at noonday.

A thousand may fall at your side,
And ten thousand at your right hand;
But it shall not come near you.

PSALM 91:1–7

For whatever is born of God overcomes the world. And this
is the victory that has overcome the world—our faith. Who is he
who overcomes the world, but he who believes that Jesus is the
Son of God?

1 JOHN 5:4–5

Let all those rejoice who put their trust in You;
Let them ever shout for joy, because You defend them;
Let those also who love Your name
Be joyful in You.
For You, O Lord, will bless the righteous;
With favor You will surround him as with a shield.

PSALM 5:11–12

And Moses said to the people, "Do not be afraid. Stand still, and see the salvation of the Lord, which He will accomplish for you today. For the Egyptians whom you see today, you shall see again no more forever. The Lord will fight for you, and you shall hold your peace."

EXODUS 14:13–14

For though we live in the world, we do not wage war as the world does. The weapons we fight with are not the weapons of the world. On the contrary, they have divine power to demolish strongholds.

2 CORINTHIANS 10:3–4 NIV

GOD PROMISES TO CALM YOU WHEN
YOU FACE DISAPPOINTMENT

In this you greatly rejoice, though now for a little while, if need be, you have been grieved by various trials, that the genuineness of your faith, being much more precious than gold that perishes, though it is tested by fire, may be found to praise, honor, and glory at the revelation of Jesus Christ, whom having not seen you love. Though now you do not see Him, yet believing, you rejoice with joy inexpressible and full of glory, receiving the end of your faith—the salvation of your souls.

1 PETER 1:6–9

We are hard-pressed on every side, yet not crushed; we are perplexed, but not in despair; persecuted, but not forsaken; struck down, but not destroyed—always carrying about in the body the dying of the Lord Jesus, that the life of Jesus also may be manifested in our body.

2 CORINTHIANS 4:8–10

But Jesus looked at them and said to them, "With men this is impossible, but with God all things are possible."

MATTHEW 19:26

Why are you cast down, O my soul?
And why are you disquieted within me?
Hope in God;
For I shall yet praise Him,
The help of my countenance and my God.

PSALM 42:11

The Spirit Himself bears witness with our spirit that we are children of God, and if children, then heirs—heirs of God and joint heirs with Christ, if indeed we suffer with Him, that we may also be glorified together.

For I consider that the sufferings of this present time are not worthy to be compared with the glory which shall be revealed in us.

ROMANS 8:16–18

The LORD is near to those who have a broken heart,
And saves such as have a contrite spirit.

Many are the afflictions of the righteous,
But the LORD delivers him out of them all.

PSALM 34:18–19

"Therefore I say to you, do not worry about your life, what you will eat or what you will drink; nor about your body, what you will put on. Is not life more than food and the body more than clothing? Look at the birds of the air, for they neither sow nor reap nor gather into barns; yet your heavenly Father feeds them. Are you not of more value than they?"

MATTHEW 6:25–26

The Lord's name is a strong tower;
    the righteous run to it and find refuge.

PROVERBS 18:10 CEB

Sing to the Lord!
    Give praise to the Lord!
He rescues the life of the needy
    from the hands of the wicked.

JEREMIAH 20:13 NIV

Hope deferred makes the heart sick; but when dreams come true at last, there is life and joy.

PROVERBS 13:12 TLB

GOD'S PROMISES IN ACTION

Which Bible promises from this section do you want to commit to memory?

....

....

....

....

What fears and uncertainties are you struggling with?

....

....

....

....

How can you deepen your relationship with God so that worry and fear don't take hold?

....

....

....

....

YOUR FUTURE IS IN GOD'S HANDS

LOUIE GIGLIO ON LIVING A LIFE OF PEACE

God is bigger and more powerful than we can ever imagine. We may be hurt, yes, but Jesus is bigger than our wounds. Jesus is bigger than our sorrows. He is able to "repay you for the years the locusts have eaten" (Joel 2:25 NIV). The things that have been destroyed by injustice, Jesus is able to restore fully.

The world tells you to hate and feel wronged and hold a grudge. But Christians are called to walk through the world with the heart of Christ. We offer people a different model. We show people a different picture, Is there a wrong in our past we're still worked up over? Hey, we've known God too long to be bitter about that. We've walked with Jesus too far to still be jacked up about this. The Holy Spirit has filled my heart too much for me to hold that grudge against you. Our God is too big for us to hate others.

Paul says in Romans 12:18, "If it is possible, as far as it depends on you, live at peace with everyone." This is the same guy who had rocks thrown at him. More than once Paul was thrown in prison. Three times he was beaten with rods. Five times he was whipped within an inch of his life. Yet he doesn't call for revenge.

He calls for peace.

—*Goliath Must Fall*[10]

How beautiful upon the mountains

Are the feet of him who

brings good news,

Who proclaims peace,

Who brings glad tidings of good things,

Who proclaims salvation,

Who says to Zion,

"Your God reigns!"

ISAIAH 52:7

GOD PROMISES TO GIVE YOU
COURAGE FOR THE FUTURE

"The LORD your God in your midst,
The Mighty One, will save;
He will rejoice over you with gladness,
He will quiet you with His love,
He will rejoice over you with singing."

ZEPHANIAH 3:17

Beloved, do not think it strange concerning the fiery trial which is to try you, as though some strange thing happened to you; but rejoice to the extent that you partake of Christ's sufferings, that when His glory is revealed, you may also be glad with exceeding joy.

1 PETER 4:12–13

Heaven and earth will pass away, but My words will by no means pass away.

MATTHEW 24:35

"For My thoughts are not your thoughts,
Nor are your ways My ways," says the LORD.
"For as the heavens are higher than the earth,
So are My ways higher than your ways,
And My thoughts than your thoughts."

ISAIAH 55:8–9

There is surely a future hope for you, and your hope will
not be cut off.

PROVERBS 23:18 NIV

Listen to counsel and receive instruction,
That you may be wise in your latter days.

There are many plans in a man's heart,
Nevertheless the LORD's counsel—that will stand.

PROVERBS 19:20–21

Come now, you who say, "Today or tomorrow we will go to
such and such a city, spend a year there, buy and sell, and make
a profit"; whereas you do not know what will happen tomorrow.
For what is your life? It is even a vapor that appears for a little
time and then vanishes away. Instead you ought to say, "If the
Lord wills, we shall live and do this or that."

JAMES 4:13–15

GOD PROMISES TO BE THERE WHEN TROUBLES COME

The LORD is good,
A stronghold in the day of trouble;
And He knows those who trust in Him.

NAHUM 1:7

So give yourselves to God. Stand against the devil and he will run away from you.

JAMES 4:7 NLV

And we know that all things work together for good to those who love God, to those who are the called according to His purpose.

ROMANS 8:28

I will be glad and rejoice in your mercy,
For You have considered my trouble;
You have known my soul in adversities.

PSALM 31:7

I will lift up my eyes to the hills—
From whence comes my help?
My help comes from the LORD,
Who made heaven and earth.

PSALM 121:1–2

The LORD is my strength and song,
And He has become my salvation;
He is my God, and I will praise Him;
My father's God, and I will exalt Him.

EXODUS 15:2

This is a faithful saying:
For if we died with Him,
We shall also live with Him.
If we endure,
We shall also reign with Him.
If we deny Him,
He also will deny us.
If we are faithless,
He remains faithful;
He cannot deny Himself.

2 TIMOTHY 2:11–13

You saw how the LORD used his tremendous power to work great miracles and bring you out of Egypt. And he will again work miracles for you when you face these enemies you fear so much.

DEUTERONOMY 7:19 CEV

"For the pillars of the earth are the LORD's,
And He has set the world upon them.
He will guard the feet of His saints,
But the wicked shall be silent in darkness.

"For by strength no man shall prevail.
The adversaries of the LORD shall be broken in pieces;
From heaven He will thunder against them.
The LORD will judge the ends of the earth."

1 SAMUEL 2:8–10

Revive me, O LORD, for Your name's sake!
For Your righteousness' sake bring my soul out of trouble.
In Your mercy cut off my enemies,
And destroy all those who afflict my soul;
For I am Your servant.

PSALM 143:11–12

GOD PROMISES THAT HE WILL NEVER CHANGE

"I am the Alpha and the Omega, the Beginning and the End," says the Lord, "who is and who was and who is to come, the Almighty."

REVELATION 1:8

"I am the vine, you are the branches. He who abides in Me, and I in him, bears much fruit; for without Me you can do nothing. If anyone does not abide in Me, he is cast out as a branch and is withered; and they gather them and throw them into the fire, and they are burned. If you abide in Me, and My words abide in you, you will ask what you desire, and it shall be done for you."

JOHN 15:5–7

The love of Christ compels us, because we judge thus: that if One died for all, then all died; and He died for all, that those who live should live no longer for themselves, but for Him who died for them and rose again. . . . If anyone is in Christ, he is a new creation; old things have passed away; behold, all things have become new.

2 CORINTHIANS 5:14–15, 17

God is not a man, so he does not lie.

He is not human, so he does not change his mind.
Has he ever spoken and failed to act?

Has he ever promised and not carried it through?

NUMBERS 23:19 NLT

"For I am the LORD, I do not change;
Therefore you are not consumed, O sons of Jacob."

MALACHI 3:6

God is light and in Him is no darkness at all. If we say that we have fellowship with Him, and walk in darkness, we lie and do not practice the truth. But if we walk in the light as He is in the light, we have fellowship with one another, and the blood of Jesus Christ His Son cleanses us from all sin.

1 JOHN 1:5-7

Then Moses said to God, "Indeed, when I come to the children of Israel and say to them, 'The God of your fathers has sent me to you,' and they say to me, 'What is His name?' what shall I say to them?"

And God said to Moses, "I AM WHO I AM." And He said, "Thus you shall say to the children of Israel, 'I AM has sent me to you.'"

EXODUS 3:13-14

GOD PROMISES YOU AN ETERNAL INHERITANCE

The LORD knows the days of the upright,
And their inheritance shall be forever.

PSALM 37:18

Blessed be the God and Father of our Lord Jesus Christ,
who according to His abundant mercy has begotten us again to
a living hope through the resurrection of Jesus Christ from the
dead, to an inheritance incorruptible and undefiled and that does
not fade away, reserved in heaven for you, who are kept by the
power of God through faith for salvation ready to be revealed in
the last time.

1 PETER 1:3–5

So now, brethren, I commend you to God and to the word of
His grace, which is able to build you up and give you an inheritance among all those who are sanctified.

ACTS 20:32

May the God of all grace, who called us to His eternal glory
by Christ Jesus, after you have suffered a while, perfect, establish,
strengthen, and settle you.

1 PETER 5:10

"Whoever eats My flesh and drinks My blood has eternal life, and I will raise him up at the last day. For My flesh is food indeed, and My blood is drink indeed."

JOHN 6:54–55

We know that if our earthly house, this tent, is destroyed, we have a building from God, a house not made with hands, eternal in the heavens.

2 CORINTHIANS 5:1

Having been justified by His grace we should become heirs according to the hope of eternal life.

TITUS 3:7

"And I will establish My covenant between Me and you and your descendants after you in their generations, for an everlasting covenant, to be God to you and your descendants after you. Also I give to you and your descendants after you the land in which you are a stranger, all the land of Canaan, as an everlasting possession; and I will be their God."

GENESIS 17:7–8

GOD PROMISES TO NURTURE HOPE FOR ETERNITY

Through the LORD's mercies we are not consumed,
Because His compassions fail not.
They are new every morning;
Great is Your faithfulness.
"The LORD is my portion," says my soul,
"Therefore I hope in Him!"

LAMENTATIONS 3:22–24

"Blessed is the man who trusts in the LORD,
And whose hope is the LORD.
For he shall be like a tree planted by the waters,
Which spreads out its roots by the river,
And will not fear when heat comes;
But its leaf will be green,
And will not be anxious in the year of drought,
Nor will cease from yielding fruit."

JEREMIAH 17:7–8

The LORD is good to those who wait for Him,
To the soul who seeks Him.
It is good that one should hope and wait quietly
For the salvation of the LORD.

LAMENTATIONS 3:25–26

May the God of hope fill you with all joy and peace in believing, that you may abound in hope by the power of the Holy Spirit.

ROMANS 15:13

Having been justified by faith, we have peace with God through our Lord Jesus Christ, through whom also we have access by faith into this grace in which we stand, and rejoice in hope of the glory of God. And not only that, but we also glory in tribulations, knowing that tribulation produces perseverance; and perseverance, character; and character, hope. Now hope does not disappoint, because the love of God has been poured out in our hearts by the Holy Spirit who was given to us.

ROMANS 5:1–5

My sheep hear My voice, and I know them, and they follow Me. And I give them eternal life, and they shall never perish; neither shall anyone snatch them out of My hand. My Father, who has given them to Me, is greater than all; and no one is able to snatch them out of My Father's hand.

JOHN 10:27-29

You are my hiding place and my shield;
I hope in Your word. . . .
Uphold me according to Your word, that I may live;
And do not let me be ashamed of my hope.
Hold me up, and I shall be safe,
And I shall observe Your statutes continually.

PSALM 119:114, 116-117

The poor shall eat and be satisfied;
Those who seek Him will praise the LORD.
Let your heart live forever!

All the ends of the world
Shall remember and turn to the LORD.

PSALM 22:26-27

GOD'S PROMISES IN ACTION

Which Bible promises from this section do you want to commit to memory?

....

....

....

....

God is in charge of yesterday, today, and tomorrow. What concerns about your future can you take to God in prayer?

....

....

....

....

What does the Bible say about the future that can help you deepen your relationship with God?

....

....

....

....

NOTES

1. Rick Warren, *God's Power to Change Your Life* (Grand Rapids, MI: Zondervan, 2006), 37–38.

2. Max Lucado, *Begin Again* (Nashville: Thomas Nelson, 2020), 68–69.

3. Craig Groeschel, *Dangerous Prayers* (Grand Rapids, MI: Zondervan, 2020), 63–65.

4. David Jeremiah, *Slaying the Giants in Your Life* (Nashville: W Publishing Group, 2001), 48–49.

5. Sarah Jakes Roberts, *Don't Settle for Safe* (Nashville: W Publishing Group, 2017), 105.

6. Christine Caine, *Unexpected* (Grand Rapids, MI: Zondervan, 2018), 41–43.

7. Lysa TerKeurst, *It's Not Supposed to Be This Way* (Nashville: Nelson Books, 2018), 94–95, 103.

8. Billy Graham, *Who's in Charge of a World That Suffers?* (Nashville: W Publishing Group, 2021), 23–24.

9. Ann Voskamp, *WayMaker* (Nashville: W Publishing Group, 2022), 197, 201.

10. Louie Giglio, *Goliath Must Fall* (Nashville: W Publishing Group, 2017), 161.

ABOUT THE AUTHOR

JACK COUNTRYMAN is the founder of JCountryman® Gift Books, a division of Thomas Nelson, and the recipient of the Evangelical Christian Publishers Association Jordan Lifetime Achievement Award. For more than thirty years, he has developed bestselling gift books such as *God's Promises® for Your Every Need*, *God's Promises® for Men*, *God's Promises® for Women*, *God Listens*, and *The Red Letter Words of Jesus*. Countryman's books have sold more than 20 million copies worldwide.